BROKEN OPEN

"Sometimes the heart must break in order to open."
— *Mark Wolynn*

"Cherishing the self comes first and caring for others is the inevitable outcome."
— *Anita Moorjani*

ACORN
PUBLISHING

info@maureentowns.com
ISBN: 978-0-9948566-9-2 (print)
ISBN: 978-1-7774018-0-1(ebook)

Ordering Information:
Special discounts are available on quantity purchases by corporations, associations, and
others. For details, contact info@maureentowns.com

TABLE OF CONTENTS

BROKEN OPEN

A MOTHER'S JOURNEY TO SURVIVE HER CHILDREN'S ADDICTION AND MENTAL ILLNESS

MAUREEN TOWNS

INTRODUCTION

A thin curtain separated Sam and I from the rest of the emergency ward. He had called me from the hospital about an hour before to tell me in a flat voice that he was okay and in the hospital after he had attempted to end his life. One of the nurses suggested he call and let me know where he was.

I rushed to the hospital, the drive a blur as my heart and mind raced. What had happened? How close had he come to dying? Thank God someone found him and he had made it to a hospital. And thank goodness one of the nurses had encouraged him to call me.

It was 2016 and not the first time Sam had attempted suicide. His last few attempts involved drinking to intoxication, then taking as much fentanyl as he could get his hands on. The opioid crisis in Canada was beginning to get media attention, and we had several family friends whose children had died from tainted fentanyl in the previous months. Each close call seemed to involve some unlikely circumstance in which he would be noticed, found, and revived.

Every one had left me breathless, reflecting on how tenuous the thread that had kept Sam alive seemed to be.

I rushed into the emergency department and was directed to where he lay behind a curtain on a narrow stretcher. There was my blue-eyed boy, now 24 years old, an IV in his arm, pale and pasty, and with specks of vomit down the front of his shirt and on the cuffs of his pants. I drew a sharp breath and tried to tamp down my shock at seeing how he looked so soon after being revived with a couple of doses of Narcan.

I leaned over and hugged him, sat down and said, "Sam, I am so glad you're still here."

He replied, "Yeah, me too."

I felt a wave of relief that he was happy to have survived. Anxious to focus more on this speck of positive light in such a dark moment, I asked, "Really?"

"No. I wish I was dead," he said flatly.

I had trouble inhaling again. I was speechless. My throat felt tight and my eyes started to sting. I swear I could feel his pain—that some of it was transferred to me in that moment. It was so deep, so raw, and so dark. It occurred to me then, in a flash, that if I felt that pain all the time, I'd want to die too.

How did we get here? This had not been part of the plan.

If you've picked up this book, chances are good that your life doesn't look anything like the one you signed up for. You've found yourself in a place you never anticipated and that you may have worked hard to avoid. You may feel that you were destined for something different. I wrote this book for you. It's designed to help you through this place by offering you some hope that things can be different.

I offer professional support as a consultant to others in circumstances similar to ours—the kind of support I wish we'd had from the beginning of our children's mental health and addictions issues. I've taken what I learned as a nurse working for 25 years in both public and private health care across Canada, my understanding of behaviour change and coaching from my master's degree in leadership studies, and my personal experience and hard-won lessons as a mother of children with mental health and addictions, and developed a path for you. I've learned how to listen to and support other parents struggling with atypical children, or children with atypical parents, or brothers with atypical sisters—families who need help. I've learned that it's difficult to love someone who's sick. Not everyone gets that.

This book is for:

- Those who feel like they're losing themselves in supporting those they love.
- Those who vaguely recall being happy and having energy but who cannot recall how to get back there.

- Those who want to be sure that what they're doing is helping and not hurting.
- Those who find themselves walking on eggshells through chaos when they desperately need calm.

Three of our four children struggled with mental health and/or addictions. Over the course of a decade, we searched for professionals to help guide us, diagnose issues, and offer effective treatment.

Sam and Ben, our eldest two, began using both drugs and alcohol at the ages of 13 and 12, respectively. The journey with treatment centres and addiction began in 2011 when Ben turned 18 years old. While Ben was in his first treatment centre, our youngest, Ally, began self-harming with cutting. It would be over a year before we knew anything about borderline personality disorder (BPD) and had an effective treatment for her. Sam experienced a psychotic break in 2012, and in 2013, we recognized his addiction as well. Weeks later, he, too, was diagnosed with BPD after one of his many attempts at suicide.

Sydney, our third child, was unassuming—she spent most of those chaotic years in her room. I call her my lost child, knowing that any needs she may have had were essentially overlooked or ignored amidst the more pressing and urgent needs of her siblings.

It was through those years of shock, shame, fear, and pain that I learned the most about how to be a better mother and more effective support and advocate for my children. Today, my relationship with them—and their struggles—is completely different than it was in those early years. I went from frantic, fearful, and controlling to calm, trusting, and empowering.

With their permission, I share our journey and the lessons I have learned along the way. And finally, I offered their father, Steve, and each of the kids the opportunity to contribute to this book. Steve declined, but you will find included chapters written by each of my four kids. I asked them to write anything they wanted the reader to know. I hope you find their words useful.

CHAPTER ONE

Our family's descent into chaos didn't start with Sam and his suicide attempts. It started with our second son's senior year of high school. Ben went from being an active, creative, engaging, and fit young teen to a lethargic, disinterested, withdrawn, and gaunt high school senior. I spent countless hours trying to figure out what was going on, what he was doing, and what made him tick. It was 2011 and my mind swirled with fears and anxieties. I worried he was becoming lazy and, as a result, would never get an education or a good job to support himself. In marked contrast to his peers, Ben didn't seem interested in a future beyond his senior year. Even though I repeatedly asked him to keep me informed about the dates and guidance the school provided to apply to universities and colleges, he missed the entire application process. His eyes would glaze over and he would leave the room at any mention of post-graduation plans.

I feared that he'd live with us forever if I couldn't find some magic solution to straighten him out. I went over different ideas to get him back on track, and I prepared for his reactions and objections. I needed to get him to take his future seriously.

I used to believe that good mothers would naturally produce good children. I had had a vision from the time I was first pregnant that my kids would be funny, intelligent, and kind people I'd enjoy spending time with.

I pictured hanging out with them as adults and laughing—we'd share the same sense of humour. They'd be interesting, and I'd be so proud to have raised them. I'd be happy to introduce them to people and beam with pride at being their mom. I'd hold a special place in their hearts and they in mine.

At 13 months apart, Sam and Ben had always been close. As we moved through their adolescences, we encountered what we considered normal teenage experimentation and rebelliousness. But at times, things seemed to border on something more serious, and their dad and I wondered if maybe they weren't so typical.

One evening while Steve was away, I came home to find both boys unconscious. They were 16 and 15 years old. An empty 40 ounce bottle of vodka was tipped over on the floor beside Sam, who was wearing only his swim trunks. His head and torso rested on the seat of a chair; his knees and feet were on the floor. A quick check told me that he was passed out drunk. I didn't see Ben anywhere, but the door to the bathroom was locked and I pounded on it. When I got no answer, I used a wooden skewer from the kitchen to pick the lock and pushed the door open an inch before hitting something solid on the floor. It was Ben's head. He was out cold on the bathroom floor, lying on his side. I could smell vomit and feces. I hollered his name and pushed the door against him until he became conscious. I managed to escort the two of them to their shared room and then sat up all night to be sure they sobered up without complications.

We were seriously concerned. Was this just a one-time incident that got out of hand? Maybe there was a problem we needed to rein in. The boys didn't seem contrite or embarrassed and our fear, anger, and concern didn't seem to faze them. This struck us as atypical too.

We wanted reassurance that all was well—we wanted to know if there was a problem or not. We wanted to be sure there wasn't some strategy we needed to employ that would get and keep them on track that we hadn't yet tried. We took the boys to the Alberta Alcohol and Drug Abuse Commission (AADAC). Later, after another incident, we brought them to a psychologist who specialized in teens. We were assured again and again we were on the right track, that we just needed to stay consistent and enforce consequences. If we did that, things would be okay. Challenging, yes, but okay in the end.

We were happy when Sam went off to university in the fall of 2010. He was a natural academic, excelling in school early on. Even as a preschooler, he had craved logic and order. He organized his toys by colour or by size. He loved puzzles. He loved math—the more complex, the better—and at five years old, he wanted to be an engineer. We didn't know any engineers then, and I have no clue where the idea came from, never mind his years of determination to follow through on it. As a high school student, he read the mathematics or calculus textbooks rather than study his notes because, he'd noticed, his teachers occasionally got things mixed up or incorrect. He found the text more reliable and would come out of his courses with perfect scores. Sure enough, he was accepted to an engineering program at the University of British Columbia.

Everything seemed right on track where he was concerned, but this wasn't the case with Ben. Ben wasn't thriving in high school, and we were increasingly concerned as he entered his last year that he wasn't going to graduate, wasn't going to go to post-secondary school—and horror of horrors, might live with us as an apathetic adult requiring our support for eternity.

Steve and I both had plenty of sleepless nights marked by restless worrying. When I lay awake, time seemed to drag. I felt very alone. I watched the alarm clock numbers change as it got later and later, and my mind raced nonstop. I was tired when I went to bed each night and hoped my fatigue would take over, that my mind would grow quiet, and that I'd fall into a much-needed sleep. I tried to relax, sometimes even holding a crystal that was supposed to help. I flipped my pillow again and again, ever in search of the cool side. I readjusted myself and tried to focus on my breathing.

But my mind always returned to the changes I saw in Ben, now 17. He'd always been a busy kid, playing outside no matter the weather, staying out in the freezing snow, enduring frozen fingers as he built an elaborate snow fort "just right." When he could convince his older brother and little sisters to join him, he became the natural leader, directing everyone to follow his vision. His excitement was contagious.

He was also a gifted athlete. He always looked his most joyous and free when running down a field with a ball, fully expressed, powerful and intuitive, enjoying his considerable speed and dexterity as he helped his team capture glory from their opponents. He would quietly dismantle anything he could get his hands on or build something from random treasures he found in our yard or garage, his face intent as he fashioned a complex structure from nothing more than an imaginary blueprint.

But in his last year of school, that boy was nowhere to be found. He'd been replaced by another who seemed lazy and lacked focus, a boy determined to avoid his family in favour of extreme partying with his friends. I'd lie awake thinking about his attendance at school, his grades, and his future. As the months went on, the scenarios I imagined shifted from what might motivate him to finish high school, go to post-secondary, or get a job to worrying that he'd be homeless, a lifelong "partier," and/or someone I wouldn't even like or respect.

I wasn't sure what the issue was or even if there was one beyond my own fear of having a son who was indifferent about a career and independence. I wanted him to yearn to be on his own, to make a living for himself and pursue a future. From what I could see, he had no interest in that—he was only concerned with what fun he could find in the moment.

Ben managed to scrape through high school, but our fears that he wasn't thriving and that things weren't going according to plan, came to fruition. Things seemed to happen so quickly but, in hindsight, the problems were there before we recognized them and certainly before we could face the devastation our lives were heading toward.

Reflective Questions:
- Are there signs that a person you love is undergoing personality changes? Is a normally supportive parent becoming manipulative? A normally active child becoming lazy and disinterested in activities they used to love? What are the things you're noticing that are causing concern?
- How are these changes affecting you and the rest of your family?

CHAPTER TWO

Some days, I decided to focus on the positives when thinking about Ben. He had, after all, graduated high school, landed a summer job, and caved in and agreed to take a part-time emergency medical responder (EMR) course in the fall, which was a step toward becoming a paramedic, a career he'd expressed an interest in pursuing. But I could not shake my concerns; he missed as many classes as he attended in his last year of high school and nothing seemed to motivate him. I prodded him with questions about his interests, and even as he said that he wanted to be paramedic, his eyes and his face would be non-expressive, almost flat. He seemed resigned as I registered him for the EMR course. He was losing weight. He'd become increasingly unreliable. The formerly gifted athlete didn't care about sports anymore. During the summer, he went out partying most nights of the week and sometimes he didn't come home at all. He eventually lost his summer landscaping job because of poor attendance. By fall, he looked sickly. He began lying more often, even about attending his EMR classes. He'd be gone for several days, only coming home when we were at work.

Throughout his last year of school, Ben denied drug use. In fact, he would tell me about other kids who used drugs and we would both lament the bad path they were on. One day, I found a pipe under the edge of our sofa. I was not even sure what it was. But I thought it smelled like marijuana. I confronted Ben. He said that he was holding it for a friend, one I had never heard of. It seemed strange but I was relieved to hear that it was not his. Relieved and naïve.

Increasingly, when Ben was at home, he would sleep for 18 to 24 hours at a time.

By October, I'd find him in bed, the sheets tangled up into a ball on the floor, lying on the bare mattress fully dressed, barely rousable. It was clear that something was wrong and when I confronted Ben, he finally admitted to being dependant on marijuana and that he was struggling to stop using.

My heart broke a little but I set a plan to help him get on track. I missed work to try to help him detox, ostensibly, from marijuana (the only drug he'd admit to using at the time), make a résumé to get a job and get cleaned up and organized. But within a few days, he'd be right back to square one: going out, staying out, and coming home when we weren't there.

I spoke with my older brother, Mike, on the phone and let him know some of what was going on. I remember the sound of my own voice saying things like, "He disappears for days, then comes home looking haggard, and sleeps for 18 to 24 hours straight. He's losing weight and avoiding us." When I heard myself saying that stuff out loud, I realized Ben's party life had gone way beyond what typical teens did. And I remember my brother's voice over the phone, his gentle questions, and then finally his assessment.

He said, "This doesn't sound good, Mo. He is definitely using a lot of drugs."

My heart sank. I felt flat as I hung up. Fear of the unknown gripped me. What could be going on? Is it still marijuana? Or something else? What does "a lot" mean? What if it's not drugs and I accuse him of that? But what else could be wrong? I had no idea. I went through the motions of life for the next couple days while trying to figure out what to do. Drugs were an unknown to me, and I didn't *want* them to be the issue. I was fearful as I let my brother's words rattle around in my head.

I was the manager of a health centre at the time. One morning at work, with the door closed, I worked up the courage to do a Google search for drug treatment in Alberta. I saw a ton of things I didn't understand— names of what I could only guess were treatment centres but no explanations about who they were for, and I felt completely overwhelmed. Where to begin? I could hear the noises of a busy office outside my door, and my heart raced as I quickly scrolled through the list of links. I was afraid of being interrupted or even worse, found out.

I was still very reluctant to believe that Ben actually had a drug problem. Those words sounded too serious. They scared me to death. I justified my denial by saying things like, "What if he doesn't have a drug problem and we say we think he does—what would that do to his self-esteem?" Under the guise of protecting him, I refused to call it addiction. At that point, I wasn't sure I could even say the word out loud; I preferred to say he was using a lot of drugs (maybe) and that he seemed unmotivated.

Of all the websites I visited that day, the one that stood out most had a large 1-800 number at the top of the screen and, underneath, the guarantee of an unbiased assessment. This number didn't seem to be affiliated with a treatment centre, which to me was reassuring—I thought I'd be more likely get an honest opinion rather than a sales pitch.

I called and was greeted by a man with a warm, friendly voice. He listened to me as the words came spilling out about how frightened I was for my son. My voice cracked, and I tried to talk in a whisper so no one in the office would overhear. Worse than anyone at work knowing what I was saying was the thought of making the call from home and having one of the kids overhear me.

I felt ashamed of even *thinking* of addiction when it came to Ben. My impression of addiction was that it was a word for people who lived on the streets, injected drugs, committed crimes, and who lived on the fringes of society. Ben had already told me that he only used marijuana—a typical teenage drug—so how could I link him to my image of a drug addict? Would it not be damaging to him to know that his own mother thought so little of him?

The man on the phone said he wanted to connect me to a treatment centre, which scared me. I asked if he thought my son really needed that, and he said he wasn't in a position to assess my son based on just this phone call—a treatment centre would be better qualified to do that. I declined. I hung up and thought I could call back if I needed to, but I worried I was taking an extreme step. I wasn't ready to talk to a treatment centre, especially not without first talking to Steve.

We continued to try to talk to Ben, motivate him, and nag him. Whenever I saw him, I'd study him closely, looking for clues as to how to get through to him. We tried the friendly collaborative approach: "Ben, we all struggle sometimes, you can do it." We tried the confrontational approach: "Ben, we didn't raise you to be a slacker. Time to get on track." And we tried the passive indifferent approach: "It's your life, and if you're not making anything of it, then you'll have to live with that." Nothing worked. Over the next weeks Ben's difficult behaviours escalated in duration and frequency.

Finally, in a last-ditch attempt to get him to buckle down and get serious, Steve and I told him he could no longer live with us.

On a Tuesday evening mid-November 2011, we told him we wanted to have a serious talk. He didn't seem overly concerned. I imagine he anticipated another lecture about getting his life on track, that he could verbally re-commit to making changes he had no intention of making and then continue living as he was. We sent the girls to their rooms and sat down with him in the kitchen. I still vividly recall facing him in a kitchen chair. He seemed upbeat but fidgety. Dressed in his usual jeans and T-shirt, he sat there and barely made eye contact. I felt like I had a brick in my stomach as Steve and I proceeded to tell him how frustrated we were. We quickly moved through the discussion—which was more of a monologue, since he just sat there listening to us—and concluded by telling him he needed to get his things and go. I expected him to get upset—to cry, to plead, to make promises in order to stay in our home—but he didn't do any of those things.

To our utter surprise, he wasn't upset at all. In fact, he seemed quite relieved as he quickly threw some things into a bag and carried his prized possessions, including his laptop, phone, and headphones to his van. We robotically pulled together some food and money. We fell all over ourselves telling him we hoped he would still come home for Sunday dinners and that we wanted to stay in contact. Before we knew it, he was driving away. We stood and cried as we watched. I don't think I slept that night or many nights in the weeks after.

Our rules had been that he needed to have a job, show up regularly to work, and pay rent to live in our home. But if he chose to go to school and attend regularly, he could live with us for free. We predicted that if he left, he would live in his van, which we'd given him a few months earlier, and recognize that surviving on your own without a job and education is tough. We were terrified and devastated that it had come to this. We had hoped he would see our support as a huge advantage.

We hoped he'd come back, ready to get serious about finding and pursuing some direction for himself.

We struggled with that decision, but we felt like we'd tried everything else and nothing worked. The disruption to our home and the rest of the family was brutal with him coming and going at all hours, to say nothing of the mess he made when he was home. Routine and any sense of peace and predictability had been elusive with Ben in our home. We had two daughters still living with us, Ally in middle school and Sydney just starting high school. Steve and I both worked full time.

I lay awake, worrying about Ben and counting the minutes until we could see him again on Sunday, since he'd agreed to join us for Sunday dinners. I worried about him getting high, falling asleep, and dying of hypothermia or aspirating. I knew of a boy back in high school who had aspirated on vomit and died after a night of drinking, and I was hearing about kids dying from opioids and those stories haunted me. I pictured Ben parked on the side of a dark dirt road and getting hit by another vehicle. There was no end to the terrible, lonely, dark, frightening fates I imagined. My biggest fear was that he would die alone and afraid. I'd take some time each day to try to find him.

The first week was hell. We quickly discovered that he frequented a neighbourhood near ours. It was a residential area that sat alongside a large cluster of big-box stores. There were lots of places for him to park and sleep overnight, and I usually found his van there or I'd spot him driving around nearby. I'd follow him to reassure myself that he was okay. The odd times that I couldn't find him, I felt lost. A few times, I found his van parked without him in it, and I'd bang on the tinted windows and holler, afraid that he was inside and hurt.

I couldn't focus at work. I couldn't be present with my other children. I couldn't talk about anything except Ben and usually just with Steve. I'd hound my other kids, asking if they'd heard from him, if he was okay. They responded in patient but annoyed tones. They were not concerned and claimed to not to have heard from Ben aside from what was on Facebook. I created a Facebook account then and tried reaching out to Ben that way but he would not respond. I was slightly reassured in that I could see that he was active online so I knew in those moments that he was alive, at least. Sam told me he thought we were overreacting and that he suspected Ben was just fine. I wanted to believe him but deep down knew that he was mistaken. I wanted Sam's assurances to assuage my own anxiety but it didn't work.

As the first Sunday neared, Ben finally responded to our texts saying he'd be home for dinner by 4:00 p.m. The table was set. Sam was away at university, so Sydney, Ally, Steve, and I all hung around the main floor of the house, a little restless as we waited. I'd made a big pot of homemade tomato sauce and loads of pasta, anxiously hoping Ben would wolf down a home-cooked meal and let his dad and I dote on him. We missed him terribly, but I thought how reassuring it would be to see that he was okay, picturing how his sisters would talk with him about what they'd been up to that week—water polo and school. But 4:00 p.m. came and went. I felt a sense of dread. What if he didn't come? Then what? Was he okay? I told myself that he was just running late—he wasn't punctual at the best of times.

We waited. His dad stood in our front window looking down the street, waiting for him to come around the corner. By 5:30 p.m., the girls were hungry. I covered the pasta to keep it warm and asked them to wait just a bit longer, vacillating between despair and anger. How could he keep us waiting with no word? We texted him to see if he was coming and if he was okay. Nothing. By 6:00 p.m., we had to admit he wasn't coming. We went ahead with dinner. We ate and the elephant in the room, our collective disappointment, kept us fairly quiet. We made some conversation but it felt strained.

I was devastated. And angry. My anger at not hearing from him fueled my obsessive search for another week or so. Steve and I both spent time, usually when we were supposed to be working, driving around looking for him. Sometimes we found him and would follow and watch him from a distance. We compared notes about how he looked—did he appear to be out of it or doing okay? We discussed what he was doing—his job at the time was climbing up on icy and snowy roofs in running shoes to provide roofing estimates. We speculated about what he was thinking—did he find his situation as desolate as it appeared to us to be, and would he want to come home soon? He appeared to become dirtier and more unkempt over the next week, but there was no sign of his being discontent with his new life of living in his van.

By that second Friday, we agreed that our plan had failed. He hadn't been shocked into responsibility and hadn't realized we'd been "right all along." We talked about what to do and had trouble landing on a plan that seemed solid. If we brought him home, what was next? By Saturday evening, as we sat trying to watch a movie with Sydney and Ally, I noted that Steve seemed as restless and distracted as I felt. I was in my pyjamas, but as we went up to bed, I asked Steve if he was open to going out to see if we could find Ben. This time, I suggested we could bring him home, even though we didn't have a plan of what to do next. It was late but Steve agreed and we drove to Ben's neighbourhood haunt. It was dark and snowing heavily. There were at least six inches of new snow on the ground.

As we pulled into the Walmart parking lot, we spotted his van pulling in at the other end. We were in luck! There he was. We watched him pull in and run over a median before coming to a haphazard stop. It was a miracle he was not noticed by the police parked nearby. It was still snowing heavily and we strained to get a good look. From about 100 feet away, we saw several people, including Ben, pour out of the van and walk into Walmart.

I assumed they were high. They looked like an intimidating group, all large men with the hoods of their dirty, tattered jackets flipped up to protect themselves from the cold.

We pulled a little closer. He'd looked bad over the previous weeks, with dirt under his nails, dry lips, and dark circles under his eyes but now he really looked homeless—raggedy clothes and shoes with no socks, even in winter, his feet slipping in and out of the leather high tops as he walked. Snow clearly went over the tops of his shoes. He had used a string to keep his pants up. Things had gone downhill very quickly.

My heart raced and I felt panicked at his rapid decline. This was our son, our little boy. I said to Steve, "Go get him."

Steve looked slightly perplexed. "What do you mean?" he asked.

I suggested quickly, "Just tell him we want him to come for a coffee and when we get him in the truck, we'll take him home."

Steve stepped out of the truck, and I watched as he walked across the parking lot and disappeared through the same door Ben and the others had gone through moments before. I took shallow breaths while I waited, my eyes glued to that door, waiting for Steve to emerge with Ben. When Steve came out the door approximately 10 minutes later, he was alone. As he walked slowly back to the truck, I could feel myself getting angry. Where was Ben? As Steve opened the truck door, I asked him that same question before he was even in his seat.

"He said 'no,' he said he was fine, and was going to stay with his friends," Steve replied. I huffed. This felt unacceptable to me. I briefly wondered if I could have convinced Ben to come along if I had been the one to go into the store. But I was unwilling to go in—I was still in my pyjamas and didn't want to face that intimidating group myself. And I don't think I could have handled his rejection either. I had to accept that Steve had done the best that either of us could do.

This was new and shocking for us. In the past, when we sat Ben down to talk about his behaviour, messes he had made, his school marks, or whatever it was, he had offered zero resistance. He would nod, agree with our points, admit to some fault, and commit to a new course of action. He was agreeable to avoid conflict—and then he would just continue with whatever behaviour he had agreed to change. While this led to a sense of helplessness on our part when it came to any kind of discipline with him, we were holding on to this agreeability and conflict avoidance to work to our advantage in this situation.

And there he was, turning away and refusing to leave this band of hoodlums to come home with his parents. We were gobsmacked, which is what motivated us to finally ask for outside help. We were clearly in over our heads; the old Ben was nowhere to be found. We were losing our son.

I had been in a fair amount of denial until this point. My own fear, ignorance, and judgement of "addiction" had kept me from taking action sooner.

Reflective Questions:
- What issue or problem are you most frightened of?
- How are you rationalizing what is going on?
- Is this rationalization an attempt to avoid looking directly at what is happening?
- At what point in your loved one's decline will you take action to find professional help for your family?

CHAPTER THREE

The following Monday, I slipped into my office, closed the door, and called that 1-800 number again. I dialed, trying to control my shaking hands and voice. The same man answered and said if we wanted to explore treatment, we should consider a centre across the country to ensure that Ben wouldn't be lured out by his friends or otherwise tempted to leave. Because Ben was 18, he'd have to do treatment voluntarily. This scared me. Ben didn't seem to want our help, or any help at all. But we had to do something. I could feel him slipping away.

Steve agreed that we should make the call to the treatment centre together, so the next morning, when the girls left for school, we made the call to Narconon, a treatment centre in Quebec. Standing at our kitchen island with the phone between us on speaker, we quickly brought the intake coordinator there up to speed.

After that first call, we hung up and looked at each other, not sure what to do. We had said we needed to discuss it before we committed to sending Ben but we were not sure what to discuss. The coordinator had said treatment far away was a good idea and it made sense to both of us. The overall cost seemed high and we were nervous about the near $10,000 we'd need to wire to get things rolling. But we also agreed that we would find necessary funds for any of our kids who needed it. We made a list of questions for a follow-up call: What were the parameters used to measure the centre's professed success rate of 80 percent? At what point in post-treatment was that statistic gathered? What was their measure of success?

I asked the question on our next call, and the intake counselor cut me off, saying, "We have the best successes of anyone in Canada." Steve and I looked at each other. It was a strange response.

We are not detail-oriented people and neither of us is naturally inclined to research. But we were afraid for Ben, and we decided that if we were to do this, it would need to happen soon. We wondered if we could get Ben to the treatment centre within a week. We'd been warned by the intake counselor that he might get used to living in his van, on the fringe of society, and that this might make it harder to get him back on track. Never mind, the counselor had said ominously, how dangerous it was to be homeless. We hung up from our second call with the number for an intervention company that Narconon had worked with. We were considering a formal intervention, like the ones we had seen on the TV show, *Intervention*, to help get Ben get to treatment.

We trusted that we'd found a team of people in the business who knew what they were dealing with and how to work together. That seemed to make sense.

Later that same day we spoke to the intervention company to set things up. When we raised the concern that we weren't sure if Ben actually had an addiction, the interventionist suggested we quit trying to determine what and how much Ben was using and just focus on the fact that he wasn't doing well.

"Are things going well for him?" he asked.

"No," we replied.

"Never mind trying to figure out if he's an addict. He's using, he's homeless, and you feel like you're losing him. That's enough."

And it *was* enough. We let go, at least for the moment, of trying to figure out what exactly Ben doing and focus instead on what we could do to try to get him back.

By Wednesday, we'd made the decision to send him to treatment, and when confirming last minute details with Narconon, they said, "We should let you know, our program is based on Scientology." Again, we paused, and considered what this meant. We quickly concluded it didn't matter to us. I knew nothing of Scientology then, except that it was an obscure religious organization when compared to Christian-based religions I was familiar with. And that Tom Cruise was reportedly into Scientology and that it had caused some friction between him and other celebrities.

At the time, I didn't care if our son came home with a set of religious beliefs I didn't share, as long as he came back happy and healthy. I didn't care—and I still don't—what religion or faith my kids identify with, not if they find solace, comfort, and in Ben's case, recovery from addiction. I had no idea what recovery would or could look like. I just wanted my son back.

We agreed to pay for an interventionist to fly to Calgary on Saturday, stay in a hotel, conduct the intervention on Sunday, then fly with our son across the country to Montreal that same day if possible. From there, Ben would go to the treatment centre, several hours outside the city, where he'd stay for about four or five months. So began the process of sending massive amounts of money to the two organizations we had hired to help us, all the while preparing to lure our son home for his intervention.

(Years later, when we found a more reputable treatment centre, they encouraged us to take our time, to consider other options, and to check their references before we decided to start treatment. There was absolutely no pressure, no defensiveness when we asked questions, and no sense of being "sold" on the program. We reflected then that Narconon had capitalized on our ignorance and on our sense of fear and urgency.)

Narconon sent a list of supplies that Ben would need in treatment so I stopped at Superstore after work on Thursday. I had a lot of feelings as I walked the aisles. I was hopeful that he'd go, afraid he might not, and worried he'd hate us. I was happy I could do this small bit of mothering for him, picking out toothpaste and deodorant. But I was also acutely aware of the contrast between the feeling of mothering and the harsh reality that we were about to blindside him with an intervention. That was the real motivation for this little bit of nurturing.

The intervention was scheduled for Sunday so I took Friday afternoon off work to write my intervention letter. The intervention company gave us a list of "must haves" for the letter. The expert said to include stories of how good our relationship with Ben used to be. What did I appreciate about him? What were some stories illustrating how difficult things had become? And how did I feel watching him slowly deteriorate? The letter ended in my ultimatum: Go to treatment or be prepared to live without my involvement or support in his life. It was a tough letter to write. I struggled to put into words how much he meant to me, and I had trouble expressing my fear and devastation at how things had gone.

Steve and I packed up the girls and arranged for them to stay with a family friend. They knew something was going on but we were vague in our responses, telling them that we had some things we needed to do that would be simpler to do if they were not home. They were surprised, suspicious, and quiet as they left for the weekend. It was hard to send them away like that without sharing the real reason why. I felt like I was lying—to the girls, to Sam, who was still away at school, and especially to Ben. We felt we had to keep all of what was going on from our other kids in case they decided to give Ben a "heads up" that we were conspiring to send him to drug treatment.

I cleaned the house because there was still that delusional part of me trying to act like we had it all together. I prepared to host my brother and his wife, who had agreed to come and help us. We'd been advised to include as many people that Ben felt close to as we could. We could trust my brother and his wife and they were like second parents to Ben, having lived with us for a time when he was young.

The clock ticked as we took each measured step toward the moment the intervention was scheduled to start —the girls left, the interventionist showed up and met with us before going to his hotel, my brother and his wife arrived and settled in, and we all prepared for the next morning. We'd told Ben that he was inheriting some money from his grandmother, who'd died the year prior and that we had papers to sign. We figured he needed the money and it was our best bet at getting him to show up.

Sunday morning, Ben arrived a half hour late and each of those minutes felt like an hour. His pupils were dilated and he seemed jumpy. I suspected immediately that he was high. He came into the house trying to greet us as if he was okay, and he cordially said hello to the interventionist and his aunt and uncle. I'm sure it started to dawn on him that something seemed strange, but he was polite and came into the living room, taking the seat we offered him. He sat quietly, looking a little confused.

The interventionist led the conversation. He told Ben that we had all prepared some things that we wanted to say to him. He then prompted the four of us to read our letters, beginning with my brother and his wife, and ending with Steve and me.

I was scared as the meeting progressed. But my confidence grew as Ben stayed calm and listened. I started to feel like he would agree to go to treatment. At the same time, I worried he'd be upset with us when he sobered up. He was friendly and agreeable at the time, but there was a knot in my stomach as I pictured him on the five-hour flight and two-hour ride to the treatment centre, all the while coming off his high and realizing we'd betrayed him. I sat and watched as he listened to his aunt and uncle, and then Steve and I, read our letters. It seemed like he could barely hear us, and I couldn't get a read on how each letter was affecting him. I looked at the interventionist, who frankly seemed bored. His job, as he had described it to us, was just "to be sure we didn't screw things up by going off-script."

After we finished reading our letters, the interventionist asked Ben if he was willing to get treatment—and he was! I savoured a moment's relief before getting back into action. I sent him upstairs to shower and put on a change of clothes. We quickly booked his flight and called the centre to confirm his landing time for pickup and transportation. We rushed him to the airport, and as we stood looking like a ragtag group in the smoking area before they went through security, my son said, with shaking hands and through cracked lips, "Thank you for caring about me."

Tears welled up in my eyes, pooled, and then streamed down my cheeks. I couldn't speak. My throat was tight and my whole body was shaking as I nodded and hugged him. He seemed grateful to us for stepping in! I'd been so afraid of so many things. What if what we were doing was wrong? What if he'd become angry? How often I thought about giving up! And all the while, Ben had needed our help and was grateful now to have it. I felt such shame and gratitude at the same time. All those difficult emotions, all that exhausting frustration, it all seemed to spill over in those tears.

We went home. But for hours, we waited by the phone, eager to get a call telling us Ben had made it to treatment safely. We were truly exhausted. The stress, worry, and emotional toll of the past weeks, of watching his decline, of worrying about him dying, then covertly planning his intervention and treatment and sending him off with a packed bag of new clothes after a quick shower—all of it had been overwhelming. I fell asleep in a chair watching TV and I slept fitfully throughout the night.

Just before the interventionist left with our son, he mentioned another organization that offered case management to help people stay sober after treatment. We couldn't think about it at the time but we set the information aside for later.

The interventionist had also given us a booklet with an uncomfortable warning. Soon after a person agreed to treatment and sobered up, things would get difficult as they began to deal with painful feelings. Typically, the booklet said, addicts exhibit a range of emotions as their recovery progresses, including anger. They also try to convince their families that they don't need more treatment and are ready to come home, and they'll make the argument from many angles—they've learned enough, for example, or the treatment centre is a bad place. If they don't get their way, they may issue threats, all in an effort to get out of doing the work involved in recovery. We had read it before the intervention and were already beginning to brace ourselves.

We were zombies by the time we finally got confirmation that Ben had settled in at the treatment centre in Quebec. It was just weeks until Christmas. We'd only shared what was going on with a handful of very trusted people; we'd only just come to terms with what was happening ourselves. Our son had been homeless, used drugs, and needed addiction treatment. I still couldn't admit he was an addict. That word seemed way too harsh. We were also dealing with reactions from Sam, Sydney, and Ally.

After their initial shock at hearing that Ben was now across the country in drug treatment, none of our other kids had much to say to us about it. They each expressed a level of disbelief that Ben was an addict, that he needed something as drastic as treatment for addiction across the country *and* that we would do all this plotting in secret. We felt that overall, they seemed a little quiet and disapproving of what we'd done and how we'd done it. I can imagine that it was traumatic for them to learn that all this had happened under their noses and to be left with feelings they didn't know how to effectively express or process. But we felt the same, like things had happened so fast, that our home had been torn apart, and we'd been thrust into lives we weren't ready to live.

I wish today that we'd slowed down, that we'd talked with people who had experienced supporting someone through treatment. Today, I know that there isn't very much separation between people who are experiencing issues like ours. Finding people who've been through it is usually just a quick chat with a friend or two away. And I wish we'd listened to our intuition that Narconon's intake coordinator's responses to questions seemed defensive and strange to us.

I wish we'd been more open with our kids about how we felt. We could have told them that we were seriously concerned for Ben without going into all the gory details. Having an open dialogue about how we were feeling would have set an example for them. They would know that they could do the same.

I wish I'd included the girls in the discussion about where they would spend the weekend instead of deciding for them and just sending them off. I wish, too, that I'd recognized that we all could have used some professional help, someone to talk to about what was going on in our home. Counselling would have done all of us a world of good.

Reflective Questions:

- Who do you trust to talk to about what is going on in your family?
- Could they put you in touch with someone, or do you already know someone who has been through what you're experiencing? Who are they? What questions could you ask them (what steps did they take, what helped, what do they wish they'd done differently)?
- After doing some research, spend some time tapping into your intuition about what feels right. Keep a journal on it, if that helps.

CHAPTER FOUR

I was in a fog the morning after Ben left for treatment. It was a sunny and cold Monday. My boots squeaked on new snow as I shovelled the porch and walkway. Ben had left his van parked on the street. I wondered what to do with it while he was away. As I neared the end of the driveway, a van pulled up and stopped in front of me. It was a neighbour I hadn't seen in months, stopping to chat. She lowered her window and greeted me with a big smile.

"Hello, stranger!" She asked what was new.

"We just sent Ben off to treatment for drug addiction," I blurted out, almost as though I was hearing it for the first time myself. I felt detached from my body as I heard my own voice and registered the expression on her face. She looked shocked and uncomfortable. The conversation ended so quickly that she drove away before she got her window back up. I stood there watching as her garage door opened and she pulled in. The street was quiet again. I turned to look at Ben's van, covered in snow.

Looking back on that day, I feel for my neighbour. I mean, how do you respond to something like that? She probably didn't know what to say or how to offer support. And I had felt slighted, as if she was avoiding me because I was a bad parent. She had kids younger than ours, and I thought she'd try to avoid us now, as if my family's crisis and our shitty parenting was a plague. As if she'd be better off spending time with people whose children were doing well. I was sure she'd want to spend time with parents who were, in short, "doing it right."

By driving away, my neighbour had inadvertently confirmed my fears that I was a bad parent. That was one of the fears that eroded my sleep. Of course, it didn't take much to believe that others thought the same thing.

"If it could happen to you guys, it could happen to anyone," one friend told me.

That was nice to hear but then he said, "In hindsight, is there anything you wish you'd done differently that might've produced a different outcome?"

The message was clear: There really *was* something we could've or should've done. We really could have prevented our son's homelessness and addiction. If I'd only been *enough*. Strong enough. Attentive enough. Loving enough. Available enough. Alert enough. Then none of this would've happened.

While there was the relief of knowing where Ben was, of no longer worrying that he was alone and dying somewhere in his van, I still didn't sleep soundly. I still lay awake most nights going over his childhood, all the way back to when he was born, wondering where I'd failed him. I wondered about his birth. When I went into labour, the back of Ben's skull was pressed against the back of my pelvis, a position known as posterior presentation. The result was a longer labour. Did that have an effect on him? I wondered about him being so close in age to his older brother, just 13 months apart, and the second of four kids in six years. Had I not given my body enough time to recover after Sam, thereby depriving Ben of some essential maternal-fetal nutrient? Had I been too busy and distracted to give him what he needed as a child? Should I have been staying home with the kids 24/7? I worried about not having Ben in enough sports—he'd been in T-ball, soccer, and school sports, but maybe that wasn't enough? Or maybe it was too much. He was a mechanically inclined kid who loved to build but his dad and I weren't—had we failed to connect with him on that level?

At the time, I felt there had to be a reason for it all. The thing that I thought about with shame and guilt most often was something his grade two teacher had said to us: Ben was a little behind on his reading comprehension. At that time, our kids were eight, seven, three, and two years old and Steve was starting a new job. Steve was a human resources executive for a large grocery company, and we'd just made the decision to move farther from our extended family to pursue the job opportunity. Steve was just settling into the gruelling hours, which were frequently more than full time. Meanwhile, I had landed a sessional contract to teach diploma nursing, and I was also pursuing a distance undergraduate degree.

Ben's teacher advised me to have Ben read aloud to me each evening so we could discuss the stories together. It was painful the few times we did it. He hated it and avoided it, and I hated it and avoided it. Not only were the assigned stories boring but our house was busy. So we didn't follow through very often on the reading aloud homework, and the issue continued to show up in his reports and in parent-teacher interviews for years afterward.

That had to be it. I couldn't stop thinking about it. I had the chance to help then and I didn't take it. That was evidence that I'd failed him as a mother. It seemed to make sense to me that his reading issues could lead to poor self-esteem, which could lead to drugs. My God, I had failed him.

Evidence suggests that blaming yourself or your spouse for a child's substance use is common and not very helpful.[1] Substance use and abuse in families have a ripple effect on not just the family but also the extended family, friends, and even the community. The best thing to do if you suspect substance abuse, or notice behavioral changes, is to have an honest discussion and seek professional assessment and help for any and all mental health issues. It's best to be as inclusive of family and friends as you can, and speak frankly and openly, identifying familial patterns in substance use and recognizing that it's not anyone's fault.[2] We'd gotten the professional assessments but I was still stuck on feeling overly responsible.

One quiet Saturday morning, Steve and I had a coffee in our bedroom. This was something we occasionally did after he returned from an early morning run; the conversations and catchups were welcome after a busy week. As we stood and picked up our cups to head downstairs, I finally mustered the courage to confess that I'd caused this mess. I hung my head and quietly told Steve what I thought the problem was. He didn't seem convinced but I was only slightly mollified.

Years later, I would understand that my obsessive preoccupation with finding a cause for Ben's struggle was about trying to find a sense of control in what felt like random chaos. If I could find a cause, then perhaps I could find a cure, a way to fix things. And I needed to fix it. My own happiness depended on it.

This was the pattern that I had always known; if I could find the way to make those around me feel better, I could feel okay. I could be safe.

I learned this early on because I was born into a home with lots of chaos.

My father's moods were volatile. When he pulled into the driveway at the end of the workday, my mom, my brothers, and I would all grow quiet, the tension among us palpable. We'd watch and listen, trying to determine his mood and, consequently, what sort of evening we'd have. If he was in a good mood and we could tread softly, it might last and we might be in for a good evening. If he wasn't, we were in trouble—there'd be tension and possibly violence.

I learned early that my own needs didn't matter. I had to stuff them down so I could pay attention to my dad instead. His needs were the most important. If I could be good enough, entertaining enough, or quiet enough, then maybe I could change his mood or fly under the radar. And then, if he got destructive, if he became abusive, maybe he wouldn't consider me a target. Sometimes that strategy worked, but sometimes it didn't. I got very good at observing people around me for clues about how they were doing and, by extension, how I was doing.

I wound up living in a hard shell to protect myself. I didn't feel much. I abhorred anything I thought was weak. I identified, naturally, as strong. My friends describe me as energetic, fun, and intelligent but also outspoken. "Tell me what you really think!" my friends would quip sarcastically after I'd unloaded my latest opinion on them. My father was equally free with his opinions of our shortcomings as kids, and the consistent messaging from him was that I was a "lazy quitter," particularly when I didn't enjoy chopping and piling wood every weekend, while my classmates were on picnics or at the mall. This accusation became firmly implanted in my brain, and I spent most of my life fearing that he might be right. So as an adult, I kept busy, and I was most comfortable when I was engaged in some kind of "action."

I began to unconsciously tie productivity and influence to self-worth so I strove for both. When things got too comfortable, I'd create a new challenge, like going back to school.

As a young mother, I continued to focus on the welfare of others. I was too busy to focus on my own needs. As a nurse, my patients, bosses, and even society lauded my concern for others. I loved "saving the day" and felt most alive when I could walk into a chaotic situation and sort things out. When I worked as a home care nurse, I'd visit newly discharged palliative patients who wanted to die at home. I'd arrive on the scene to find a frightened and disorganized family and a patient whose pain was often out of control. I organized supplies and established a system to control and manage the patient's pain. I'd get the patient settled and set up the schedule for nursing visits. The family would follow me out to the car with an appreciative "Thank you, nurse." I could almost feel an invisible cape and boots; I was a superhero, and I'd saved the day. It was a total rush, a codependent's dream come true. (By codependence, I am referring to that behavioural trait in which one person has an excessive reliance on other people for approval and a sense of identity. That was me.)

On that sunny and snowy morning after Ben went to treatment, as my neighbour drove away, the load I had been carrying—that belief that I was responsible and had failed—could have been lightened a little with some support that I didn't know how to ask for.

Reflective Questions:

- Many of us tend to believe that we could or should have done something differently when we, our loved ones, or our families are in trouble. How is this statement true for you? What is false in this statement?
- If you were your own best friend, what would you tell yourself about those beliefs/regrets?

Endnotes

1   https://www.cbsnews.com/pictures/teen-drug-abuse-14-mistakes-parents-make/2/

2   https://www.ncbi.nlm.nih.gov/books/NBK64258/

CHAPTER FIVE

When someone you know is struggling with their child—and we all know someone who is—there are things you can do to lessen the self-reproach I guarantee they feel. You can learn how to "hold space" for them and listen. It sounds simple, and it is, but it's not easy. We all want to "know what to say" and make things better; we all want to clear-cut our forests of pain. We want to quickly rid others—and ourselves—of the discomfort of negative thoughts and emotions. Pain can be intense, and your friends who are suffering may be looking for answers you don't have. But I'm here to tell you that even though you don't have answers and you can't fix it, you can offer help and support, just by listening.

The concept of holding space is that you, as a listener, do just that—sit with people and listen. You become present with your whole self. You sit with them, or walk with them, and listen unconditionally and without judgement. You don't try to direct them, or fix them, or steer them in any direction; you let them lead and go where they go. You let go of your own thoughts and judgements and accept people wholly for who and where they are in that moment. Again, this is not complicated; it's quite simple. But it's not always easy.

The trick is to remain present. You don't want to take on your friend's pain, and you don't want to make them feel like they need to justify that pain. You can feel it with them but you need to recognize that it belongs to them—that it's okay and it's temporary. Try not to take it on as your own. Remind yourself that other people's feelings are theirs and that your feelings are yours.

It can be hard to stay healthy when offering companionship to people in pain, so it's helpful to take measures to look after your own mental health. You can do that through, among other things, journaling, meditating, exercising, getting enough sleep, and ensuring you're eating and drinking the foods your body needs.

Remind yourself you are not responsible for making that pain go away.

Alternatively, when sharing your own pain, be careful to share with someone who doesn't seem eager to jump into drama. There are people who seem to love "being in the know" and people who seem to relish other people's emotional pain, perhaps as a strategy to avoid their own. We all know people who are too eager to hear about what's going wrong. It's one thing to hold space for someone who's suffering, it's another to spend time around people who feed off drama. Choose wisely.

The practice of holding space requires empathy. You have to be fully present with someone and willing to connect with feelings in yourself that match the other person's feelings. And you have to *express* those feelings. It looks like active listening, which means eye contact, matching body language, and letting the other person speak without interruption. Then after someone has shared, you express a feeling related to what you've heard, such as, "That sounds really tough. I can imagine how you could feel [sad, hopeless, angry]." It's about letting someone know they're not alone. It's about validating and normalizing their feelings. And it leads to a feeling of connection.

This is what I needed as I was shoveling my walk the morning after my son went to treatment. But I didn't know about it. Even if I had, I wouldn't have known how to ask for it or where to find it. Still, it would've helped me work through the shock, the shame, and the self-doubt. Instead, I felt judged, shamed, and utterly alone. I worried that I'd overshared with my neighbour. I learned quickly to keep my mouth shut.

I craved someone who knew what it was like, even though I would have avoided any support groups had I known about them. I had a bias that support groups were filled with people who complained a lot. I know today that this is not true and that a support group would have done me a world of good. I desperately wanted reassurance that I was a good mother. And I needed someone to recognize that I'd done everything I could, everything I knew how to do. I'd worked really hard to be the person my kids needed. I hadn't *just* done my best—I wanted to hear that I'd done as well as *anyone* in my shoes could've done. I wanted to hear that I was going to be okay, that my son was going to be okay, and that someday we'd be a family again.

I understand no one could've told me that. But someone could've listened as I expressed my utter sadness, my anger, my desperation, my hope, my shock, and my fear, and someone could've told me it was okay to have those feelings. I needed someone to tell me that I *was* a mom who tried her best and that what I'd been faced with as a mother wasn't just unusual—it was really hard.

That would've been nice.

When we finally did find help, it was at an adolescent treatment centre in Alberta almost two years later. This was our second experience with drug treatment, and we were told here that our kids weren't "normal" or typical; they had serious illnesses and needed help that parents could not, and should not, try to provide. We were told there was help, not just for our kids but also for us. We were told that no parent is perfect and that if love was enough, our kids would've been fine. This all helped tremendously, and I did eventually learn to ask for what I needed. And how to find those who could provide it.

Learning to ask for what you need means learning to get in touch with how you feel. It requires comfort with accepting things as they are and refraining from the compulsion to take action to change it. It requires comfort with being still. It means you have to reach out and be okay with someone reaching back.

Consider any time you've vented to a friend or told a story about a situation that bothers you. Surely, you've experienced that same friend trying to fix things by offering advice on what you "should do." When this happens, are you aware of, or present with, whatever it is you're feeling? You might feel relief because advice is what you wanted and the advice you're getting is spot on. But often, people complain about that kind of advice. Often, *all* they want is someone trusted to lend an ear. Sometimes all people want is to share where they are, without it being made wrong, without it becoming a problem or something to "fix." And if that's what you want, then it's up to you to ask for it. You need to tell your friend exactly what you need. When you find someone who can offer that without judgement, then you're on your way.

Since then, I've learned that even when someone is suffering and in shock over a situation I haven't experienced, I can still hold space. I can still listen. I can validate and empathize. I can say things like, "I don't know what to say. You don't have to go through all this alone. I'm here and can listen to you as long as you need to talk." And I've learned to hold people's confidence.

I remember hearing from a friend that my neighbour had shared our story with her, I think, in an effort to "call in the troops" for support, but it felt like we were the subject of gossip and that was hard. If I want to call in the troops for someone, I ask permission first. And I'm careful and very selective to find non-judgemental people to reach out to. It's important to discriminate when you share, whether on your own behalf or on behalf of someone you care about. Even today, when someone asks me if I know what's going on with so and so, when someone tells me they're just worried, I play it safe. Unless I have permission to share, I say I don't know what's going on. That's what I would want.

In summary, these are the ways that you offer true support to your friends:

- Hold space: Be present with the person. Allow them to talk, feel, and think without trying to change any of it. Resist the natural urge to make things "better" or to solve their problem.
- Listen: Stay quiet about your own thoughts unless asked. Allow your friends to lead and direct their stories about what's happening in their lives. Resist the urge to provide your thoughts or talk about the time when you felt or experienced something similar (i.e., making it about you, not them).
- Keep the person's confidence: Consider everything people tell you confidential. Ask permission before, not after, sharing information with someone else.
- Look after yourself: Take time to journal, exercise, laugh, eat well, sleep, or whatever else brings you joy. When *your* needs are met, you can be generous in spirit and in meeting the needs of others.

There's a quote I recently read on Glennon Doyle's Instagram. She is an author and philanthropist in recovery from her own addictions. It reads:

"We think that our job as humans is to avoid pain, our job as parents is to protect our children from pain, and our job as friends is to fix each other's pain. Maybe that's why we all feel like failures so often—because we all have the wrong job description of love. People who are hurting don't need Avoiders, Protectors, or Fixers. What we need are patient, loving witnesses. People who sit quietly and hold space for us. People to stand in the helpless vigil of our pain."

CHAPTER SIX

By Christmas, we felt terribly guilty for having sent Ben away for the holidays, even though we knew that he couldn't have continued living in his van. We felt conflicted. We'd always been together as a family and had a great time over the holidays. It felt a little like we'd sent our son away to be alone while the rest of us celebrated together. In an effort to normalize a very abnormal situation—an effort I'd make more than once in the coming years—we bought hundreds of dollars worth of gifts and paid another several hundred in shipping to send the package across the country. It was important to us that Ben feel like he was part of our celebration, and we jumped through many hoops trying to arrange a Skype call on Christmas Day. We did get through to him on Christmas Day. It was awkward, and short, but at least we had some sense of togetherness.

By mid-January of 2012, and as predicted by the intervention company, Ben started calling to complain about the facility and staff, saying that they were using drugs themselves, or that the clients were left unsupervised, or he'd tell us he'd learned his lesson and that he would be better off at home. These were tough calls to get, but Steve and I agreed we were doing the right thing in leaving Ben to finish the program. But there was a part of me (and likely Steve too) that wondered about the place. Was it safe? Was he getting the treatment he needed? Was there some truth to what Ben was saying? Would he have really been better off at home?

At about the same time, I got a call one evening from my youngest daughter's boyfriend's mom. She said she was worried about Ally. Her son had told her that Ally was cutting herself and had threatened to kill herself via text message while they were arguing. I tried to stay calm and listen, but inside I could feel my adrenaline kick in. In the moment, I thought Ally's behaviour was inexcusable, and I quickly judged it as an attempt to get attention. Why did she have to be so dramatic? Why did she have to act out like this? But I also wondered if I should be concerned that it was maybe more than an attention-seeking ploy, more than just simply acting out. I hung up the phone and raced up the stairs to talk to Ally, then just shy of 14 years old.

Ally was a quiet girl who'd always done things on her own terms. When I wanted her to learn to swim, she obstinately refused until years later, when she took to the water like a fish. When I wanted her to learn to ski, she resisted, only to tuck and race down the slopes a couple years later. Ally always seemed to bond with strangers easily. When she was a toddler, Steve and I joked that she was adopting other families at the beach, the store, or wherever she found new friends to chat with. She always related well to both kids and adults, an old soul from an early age.

Looking back, I would say that Ally has always been able to see through a person's carefully constructed facade into their deeper interior and she does this without judgement. She connects to a person's best self—their core. Today, if I catch her at work in her customer service job, I notice her eye contact, her piercing observation, and ability to connect with her clients. It all stands out and makes her good at what she does. During those fragile teen years, I think Ally struggled when she didn't find her easy and unconditional willingness to connect with others reciprocated and she felt alone.

But on that evening, I wasn't thinking about those qualities. She was scaring me a little and embarrassing me a lot. Ally confided that she had indeed cut her forearms. She showed me her text history. Sure enough, she'd sent some messages that were concerning, but she reassured me that her self-harm wasn't an attempt to kill herself. Then we talked about how inappropriate it was to threaten to hurt yourself when someone behaves in a way you don't like. This was emotional manipulation and it wasn't okay. Then I had a look at her arms. I saw a few cuts and I felt ill. How could my little girl do this to herself? And at the same time, I was angry; I was afraid for her but could not face that fear.

It can be said that anger is fear's bodyguard and in this case it was true. I projected my fear onto Ally as anger because I didn't know what else to do with it. I told her to stop and I hoped it would end there.

But the cutting continued so we set up an appointment with the family doctor. We needed some support.

Ally was referred to psychiatric care (the waitlist was about eight to 12 months), and in the meantime, our family doctor advised that the quickest way to get help was to present to an emergency department or urgent care for a fast-track referral to youth mental health. We did that, and Ally surprised us by being excited about her appointments with a nurse counsellor and a consulting paediatric psychiatrist who visited Calgary about once a month. We attended those appointments for the better part of a year, with no noticeable improvement. There'd be short periods of time in which we would think there was progress—Ally would verbalize feeling better and the cutting would decrease for a time. But things would invariably revert to Ally feeling overwhelmed and she would self-harm again, with more intense cutting, over more areas on her body. Again, I was horrified, and I felt ill when I saw the extent of the harm, the harsh, red, raised cuts on her beautiful skin.

Increasingly, I spent time awake at night wondering what rules I could enforce that would keep Ally from harming. Would it be random body checks? Would the fear of being found out stop her? Or would it be random bedroom checks for sharps or bloody Kleenex? Would that make her think twice when she was tempted to cut? I resolved to try and find the "thing" that would keep her from cutting herself.

I now know that self-harm is a behaviour used to cope with overwhelming negative feelings that is often followed by a return of those negative feelings and shame. It's an indication of emotional pain, not typically an indicator of suicidal tendencies.[3]

It startles me today to consider how little understanding I had of what she was going through and as a result, how little I knew about how to help her. One of the important aspects of the work I do today with families is to help them to find empathy for the person who is struggling, in addition to finding empathy for themselves. Empathy and understanding for someone who is struggling can help family members let go of anger and frustration and find connection, which ultimately builds the trust that is essential in a supportive relationship.

Reflective Questions:

- Can you imagine what it would feel like to live in the skin of the person in your life who is struggling?
- Imagine for a moment what it must be like to be driven to do something harmful to yourself or your family or be unable to avoid a behaviour that is causing you and your family so much conflict/tension.
- Where can you find information about what your loved one is experiencing?
- Is there a resource available from someone who has experienced the same thing that helps you to understand the subjective experience of their struggles?

Endnotes

3   https://www.nami.org/About-Mental-Illness/Common-with-Mental-Illness/Self-harm, https://www.mayoclinic.org/diseases-conditions/self-injury/symptoms-causes/syc-20350950

CHAPTER SEVEN

Staff at Narconon, Ben's treatment centre in Quebec, was difficult to contact. Sometimes there was no answer. Sometimes there was an answer, but I was told that there was no one person who was overseeing Ben's treatment and, therefore, no one person for me to talk to. I could not get a handle on how the organization was structured. We couldn't tell if they were putting us off or if maybe there was a language barrier that made them seem unduly distant (the centre was in a small town in Quebec that spoke predominantly French). We sent money every week to Ben's "spending account" so he could buy cigarettes and incidentals when he and the other addicted clients were escorted to a store in the small town. Ben went through an awful lot of spending money and we couldn't help but wonder if that was legitimate. Did he really need all this cash? Was he getting high? Was he buying things for other clients at the treatment centre? There didn't seem to be a way to get solid answers. The expenses seemed endless, and my fear that the treatment wouldn't work silently brewed with my resentment at the costs.

Steve and I decided to book some time to fly out to see him. We arranged to go at separate times so one of us could be home to hold down the fort. I was the first to head out. In February, I flew to Montreal, rented a car, and drove to a hotel several hours away. I found the treatment centre and went to pick Ben up on the day pass I'd arranged the week prior. The centre was outside the small city of Trois Rivières, across the road from a penitentiary. I drove into what was supposed to be the Narconon parking lot, wondering if I had the wrong address. Could this really be it? It was run down, remote, and nothing like the photo on the website. And although I could feel eyes on me as I parked and got out of my vehicle, I couldn't find the main entrance.

I wandered through a door and down the hall and I couldn't help but wonder, what's stopping people from coming and going? Was there security to make sure that the clients were safe or to make sure drugs weren't brought in? I remember reading a strict code of conduct that forbade men and women from fraternizing, yet here I was wandering around freely. Eventually, I found a security guard and he tracked my son down for me.

As Ben came toward me, I took in his weight gain, his clear blue eyes, and his big but tentative smile. He looked like the old Ben and my pent-up anxieties and worry slipped away. I had been asked to sign a paper saying I'd have him back by 10:00 p.m. Again, finding someone at the facility who could or would speak to me about his recovery seemed impossible. The only official I could find was the security guard.

A few clients were visible as we headed to the car. They were openly curious as we left the grounds. Ben pointed them out and told a few stories about some conflicts between other clients that had turned violent. His recollection seemed to border on sensational and he said the conflicts arose from challenged egos. This reminded me of the type of conflict I'd seen in prison movies. Ben emphasized that he'd "get out of the way" and avoid conflict of any kind, especially with the tougher and more volatile clients. These were middle-aged men I was looking at, tattooed and with thick necks, and Ben seemed out of place among them. He was still filling out as an adult male and here he was with these hardened, tough-looking, and sinister men who were reportedly violent! Could this really be what was best for him? Was it working? Was all adult treatment like this?

I had nothing to go on. I hoped this was all an exaggeration; Ben had always been good at telling tall tales. But these men looked like people I'd avoid on the street. And Ben was supposed to be getting healthier in this environment? Things felt a little off, but again, I didn't know if this was the best we could expect.

We went out and had a good visit, however strained. My relief at seeing him earlier was short-lived. He recounted rather colorfully how the first few weeks were spent detoxing in a sauna for hours at a time to "sweat out all the drugs." I didn't know what to think. I remember watching him drink a pot of coffee loaded with sugar. He was acting hyper and high, and I was concerned. Even though he looked better physically, he didn't seem well. I asked about the spending money—was he really using it all for cigarettes and candy? He admitted giving away a lot of cigarettes to friends who could not afford their own! I asked him to stop doing that—we could not afford it either.

It seemed like there was no regulation or oversight. How could the counselors not notice one of their youngest clients being manipulated into purchasing things for other adults in the program? I quietly resolved to put a cap on what we put into his account. Again, I wasn't sure what to expect from a treatment centre, what might be a good or bad sign, so I continued to trust that we were on a positive path.

I was relieved to head home a few days later, after which it was Steve's turn to go see him. He came home with many of the same impressions that I did.

When I think back, I shake my head at how much time, energy, and money we spent trying to make Ben's drug treatment palatable. We were demonstrating our love for him by going to these lengths, or so we thought. But now I consider that maybe it was really ourselves we were trying to reassure and it was *us* we were trying to make feel better.

By March, we knew we were nearing the end of Ben's treatment but we didn't have a firm date. Ben told us that his "graduation" would be an event marked by the facility and that family wasn't involved. He also told us that graduation would happen when they determined he'd completed his work but no one was too sure when that would be. Ben told us it would be sometime towards the end of April. This was exciting but also very scary. We couldn't help but imagine Ben back home and that was worrisome. I worried about his socializing with his old friends who still used drugs. I worried about him going out at night and not coming home. I worried about his not having a job and, as such, too much time on his hands. Everything I worried about would lead him to his old behaviours. How could we be sure he'd be safe once he was back home?

Steve and I wondered if perhaps it would be wise to call the profes-sionals at that California company the interventionist had mentioned. We thought we had a month or two to investigate their services and potentially get things set up but, as it turned out, we didn't. Things were about to take a fast turn.

I got a frantic phone call from Ben while I was at work one day in early April. "The centre is being shut down and all the clients have to be out of here in a few days," he told me. He said people were being shipped off to other centres or just cut loose. Could this be real? Or just another of Ben's attempts to get us to bring him home? I left work to try to get in touch with a staff member at the centre. Our son was due to finish the program in a few weeks and we'd been waiting to hear about a date so we could arrange for the transition, but now we were suddenly being told he might be coming home immediately. It sounded wildly unlikely.

I finally reached a staff member and learned that the centre was indeed being shut down because of a failure to comply with provincial regulations regarding medical detox. Steve and I were frantic, and we were fuelled by fear that night as we searched for flights.

We found ourselves thrust headlong into the tense, frightening process of flying across the country to bring Ben home, even as we weren't quite ready to have him back. We were already nervous about the transition home and hadn't had time to put a plan in place to facilitate the process. It sounded like every client was in an abrupt, every-man-for-himself dis-charge situation.

But was Ben ready to come home? How could we make sure he stayed sober? What could we do if he didn't? What expectations were realistic? What rules could we impose? These questions cemented our decision to hire the group from California that had been recommended by our in-terventionist from Chicago. So we called and rather than inquire, we just went ahead and hired a drug counsellor to fly from California to Calgary and stay with us for a week.

"We do the worrying for you so that you can relax," the company told us, and that was all we needed to hear at that point. We were afraid, and anyone promising to take away that fear was hired!

After a nerve-wracking and expensive evening booking last-minute airline tickets, I once again flew five hours to Quebec. And once again, I drove the two hours to the treatment centre. I arrived after dark the next day so tense that I ached everywhere. I looked around the outside of the building but there didn't seem to be anyone there—until the silhouette of a large man materialized from the dark. Ben had said there were hardly any staff left and that the clients, some of whom were relapsing, had the run of the place. It crossed my mind that this could be a sick man looking for trouble. I steeled myself for conflict, which, oddly enough, would've been a kind of relief—I was so incredibly angry and filled with adrenaline.

But the man wasn't an addict. He was a security guard, the only staff member left, from what I could tell, and he helped me find my son. When he led me to Ben, I felt a wave of relief. I realized then how worried I'd been, and I felt a desperate urge to get him out of there as quickly as possible. We packed in a hurry. I was aggravated. I thought he'd be ready to go. Everything seemed to be in chaos. Ben was a little jittery and seemed unusually forgetful to me. I was concerned. He didn't seem all that recovered and healthy. While he had gained weight, he wasn't the calm, centered boy I'd hoped to be taking home.

We were on separate flights and we both had to make connections before our destination in Calgary. I was terrified he wouldn't make it. He seemed fragile to me. I was afraid he'd wander off somewhere, find drugs and get high, and miss his flights. I held my breath for much of that day until he finally landed in Calgary and we met up again. When we did meet up, he confided that he'd lost his passport in the Toronto airport on his layover, that someone had found it, and that he'd been paged over the intercom to come and retrieve it. It really had been a tenuous journey!

All in all, 34 patients and families were affected by Narconon's abrupt shutdown. About half were sent to other Scientology programs in the United States, and the rest really were simply let go to find their own ways.[4]

Ben was left somewhat disillusioned after the shutdown. The main impact was, he said, that he realized that not all adults knew what they were doing! On the bright side, he said Narconon taught him that he was not alone—that there were other people like him who struggled.

I offer tips in Chapter Thirteen about how to shop for a treatment centre. I want to offer some reflection here on the experience with our first one: I had some misgivings when Steve and I were initially talking to Narconon on the phone about their success rates and then again when I flew out to visit. Also, throughout Ben's stay, I had difficulty finding a staff member to talk to me about what was happening there. Each time I had a sense that something was not quite right, I mentally shrugged and told myself that I just didn't know anything about treatment and that maybe this was to be expected, even though I had, by then, many clues that this centre was not reputable.

The main point I want to make here is that if you're having misgivings, listen to them and do more research!

Endnotes

4   https://www.cbc.ca/news/canada/montreal/scientologist-run-rehab-centre-or-dered-closed-in-quebec-1.1226881

CHAPTER EIGHT

Ben and I arrived home after dark and I steeled myself for the week of transition ahead of us. I felt relief at making it home with Ben but that quickly gave way to fatigue and a strong feeling of anxiety about Ben's reintegration.

The next morning, Richard, our new drug counsellor, arrived on our doorstep. He was in his forties, a trendy dresser, and I wondered how he would connect with Ben. He planned to spend the week with us to help get Ben, just 18, settled into a routine and to set up a life that included drug counselling and random drug testing.

Richard helped us make a sobriety contract for Ben and helped him reconnect with the landscaping business he worked for before he became homeless. We set up remote counselling and monitoring, which Ben resented. Richard also convinced Steve and I to try Al-Anon meetings, a meeting for friends and family members of alcoholics, and he persuaded Ben to go to Alcoholics Anonymous (AA) meetings with him. Ben didn't believe he was an alcoholic, which had been reinforced in Narconon; they advised him to avoid his drug of choice (MDMA or Ecstasy), but they'd also said he could likely use alcohol and be just fine. This was a concern to us and to Richard, who believed that all drugs and alcohol were a problem to addicts. Ben had no interest in AA's 12-Step program, which is all about surrendering to a higher power. This was foreign to him. It seemed contrary to the Scientology-infused program, which relied heavily on will power.

Ben described the exercises and work that he did at Narconon—hours of staring into another person's eyes and trying to remain focused and emotionless. It sounded like practice in self-control. He showed us his workbooks, which appeared to me to be very juvenile, with cartoon illustrations. The tone of the books was "just say no" to things that would not make you a success and "yes" to things that would. Richard frowned when he looked at Ben's workbooks, and when I asked him if they were typical of drug treatment, he seemed to be struggling to find words that would indicate what he really thought while allowing him to stay tactful. I don't recall what he actually said, but I was left with the impression that Richard, coming from a 12-Step background, thought that Narconon was a waste of time and money. While I didn't know much about addiction and recovery, I sensed that it was more complex than just saying "no" or Ben would have already been healthy. I wondered, is this what we paid for?

For us, the 12-Step program we found in Al-Anon seemed out of place. I thought that the 12 Steps were *just* for addicts; we had no idea how a 12-Step program would help us as parents. Then I had an idea! Perhaps, the 12-Step poster we saw at the Al-Anon meeting was a reference so that we could see what our addicted family member was supposed to be doing in AA. It all felt very new and very foreign.

During the week, Richard convinced me to go to an open AA meeting with him and Ben while Steve was at work. We chose a meeting in a lower-income area of the city because Richard seemed to think it would expose us to a more raw and authentic show of what the program could do. When I called up the list of meetings, he asked if there was a place in the city that might have "biker types." I shrugged and pointed to this area, and he nodded, saying yes, this would be a good meeting for us.

I sat in a folding chair in a cluttered church basement and listened to an alcoholic tell his tale. I could see an old woman in a worn pink winter coat waving at me from the corner of my eye. She was trying to get my attention as I listened to the speaker, and I was quietly incensed at her rudeness. Didn't she have any manners? Couldn't she manage her own impulses long enough to wait until the end of the meeting? This went on intermittently for the full hour. I left the meeting shaking with anger.

Why had this woman's behaviour and the meeting itself gotten under my skin so acutely? In that moment, I was angry with Ben for being an addict, and I was angry at being dragged into a situation in which I felt forced to sit and deal with people I found so off-putting. I was shaking as we pulled away from the curb after the meeting.

As I thought more about it, I realized why the woman's behaviour bothered me so much. She reminded me of my alcoholic grandparents.

Growing up, I had hated going to functions at my father's parents' home. Even as a young child, I knew I wanted nothing to do with the emotional outbursts, the sloppy drunks, the volatility. But my grandparents didn't have to be drinking to lack social skills. They certainly didn't relate well to children and I remember not trusting them. When we were all together, there was always a scene involving my grandparents: Nana falling into the Christmas tree, either one starting an argument, Grandpa passing out in his plate at dinner. It was scary.

I looked forward to the day I could avoid the shortcomings of my emotionally volatile extended family. I watched as my grandparents caused drama in my parents' lives and by extension, my own. I hated that they had such reach. When I was old enough, I avoided them. I would spend my adult life striving to avoid people like them. What put me off wasn't the alcohol—after all, Steve and I drank and had a great time with my brothers and their wives—but I couldn't stand the emotional outbursts and poor impulse control; they seemed manipulative, ignoring social cues and boundaries, and this was a real trigger. I didn't know how to handle it.

At the meeting in the church basement, I found myself with other alcoholics who didn't seem able to control their impulses, who seemed to be on the verge of outbursts, and whose behaviour I felt obliged to put up with until I could get away. It was like being right back in those frustrating and frightening situations from my childhood.

Over the years, I'd worked so hard to make sure I could avoid people like this. I got an education, moved into a middle- to upper-income neighbourhood, and worked with Steve to raise our kids with some sense of emotional stability and social accountability. I became a nurse-manager in a marginalized area of the city, and I worked with clients who sometimes reminded me of my grandparents but that was okay: I felt like my position afforded me a comfortable degree of separation and choice. I believed I could create a life "better than" the one I'd spent so much time and energy running away from. As such, I felt victimized by Ben and his addiction, which I felt had returned me to a past I'd worked so hard to escape.

My feelings about my family of origin were not Ben's fault. And my fears were not his fault either. Separating my sadness and fear for Ben from my sadness and fear as a child was tough but it has been critical in gaining perspective on my kid's lives today. Carrying that baggage of my childhood and the fears associated with it left me with a narrow and rather uncompromising view of how my kids needed to live and how they needed to "turn out." I put a lot of pressure on them, and on me, to ensure that their lives unfolded in a certain way, dodging anything that reminded me of what had scared me as a kid.

Richard's desire to attend a meeting in a lower-income neighbourhood to expose us to a gritty and unfiltered population in AA is a technique I've seen used over and over again since. There seems to be a belief that people lacking a filter are somehow more "real." I didn't need more "real." I come from unfiltered, and I wanted nothing to do with it and refused to welcome it into my family, my home, my middle-class neighbourhood, and my professional career.

It would be years before I'd see my own arrogance, my own self-righteousness. That lady who reminded me so much of my nana helped set me on that path. But in that moment, all the freedom I'd worked for—the freedom from my past—had been ripped out from under me, like a cheap magic trick in which someone pulls out the tablecloth and everything crashes to the floor. This was how my life was shaping up.

I had set the table carefully and now it was crashing to the floor.

Reflective Questions:
- What are you having strong emotional reactions to in the present? What from your past does this remind you of?
- What is different about your situation today than the past that you're reminded of?

CHAPTER NINE

None of us wanted to go back to AA. Ben had come home from Narconon with the idea that he should stay away from Ecstasy and MDMA but that he would be able to drink alcohol and live, in his words, "like a normal 18-year-old." But our contract with him stipulated complete sobriety and that's what we thought was necessary.

He was not interested in, or committed to, complete abstinence so within a few weeks of being home, he began partying and drinking again. We were discouraged and heartbroken. We felt we had no choice but to ask him to move out. And he did, leaving in his van again.

We wondered if it had all been a waste of time and money and if this was what we could expect for the rest of our lives. Was the treatment centre terrible? Or was there no solution to the problem? Things felt bleak and hopeless.

Once again, we were dealing with a son who was using and couldn't live at home, only now we were in debt as well. Ben was on his own, using alcohol and possibly drugs, and we had spent just over $100,000 on his recovery to date. When we reflected on where we had ended up, we felt like we'd done our best but also like we'd been sold on bogus interventions. We'd had no idea what constituted a good or bad decision in choosing treatment centres and no idea what other options existed. Our decisions had been fuelled by fear and urgency. Part of the urgency was concern that Ben was living on the street but, honestly, some of it was me: I'd been anxious to get him looked after, not just for his sake but also so I could stop obsessing over him. Making a move, even a hasty one, was better than living in perpetual chaos and fear. Something was better than nothing, and I had anticipated a feeling of relief after sending him to treatment. I wanted to sleep a little more soundly and to refocus on ourselves and our other children.

Things didn't feel normal while Ben was in treatment but at least I didn't constantly worry that he was dying somewhere, cold and alone. There was some relief in that.

Asking Ben to leave the second time was relatively drama-free. He couldn't meet our conditions for living with us and left without a fuss. There was a stipulation that he was welcome to visit anytime but only if he was sober. The place that he moved to was, by all accounts, a little dodgy. He lived with a couple he described as young and in an abusive relationship. He said they used drugs and alcohol on a regular basis and fought in front of him. He described getting pulled into the drama. The young woman would "confide" in him and, according to Ben, seemed to want protection, yet she was willing to continue living in a circular pattern of abuse and manipulation. I felt sad when I thought about Ben living there, and I was disappointed with how things had ended up. I couldn't believe this sort of drama and dysfunction had become the norm for my son. I'd think, "My God, you're being manipulated and pulled into other people's messes." It felt hopeless to me that Ben would ever be healthy. Once again, I was reminded that he was surrounded by people I had worked hard to keep him away from.

When I first went to Al-Anon that April, I learned about the three Cs: You didn't cause it, you can't control it, and you can't cure it. I was desperate to believe that. I'd been torturing myself about Ben for well over a year. I could see relief in believing I wasn't the cause but I was secretly suspicious. Was this just some platitude designed to make us parents feel better? In those meetings, I heard other parents searching for a cause to their child's suffering and by extension, to their own suffering. And as an outsider, I could see the absurdity in the links they made between their parenting (like letting their kids quit piano or allowing too much spare time in their schedules) and their children's addictions. But just like me, those parents were convinced that something they'd done, or not done, had sowed the seeds of addiction and chaos.

Steve and I began to attend Al-Anon meetings regularly, and although I didn't yet understand the principles of the program, I found great comfort in the group. I enjoyed the connection to people who understood firsthand the fear and chaos we lived in. But there was also a part of me that went to those meetings hoping to hear about how to better manage Ben's addiction. One night, I heard a woman share and I swear she told my story.

Her son was an addict. He lived with her and it was wearing her out. She talked about his history living on his own and the pain in watching him struggle, then the turmoil of him moving in and out of her home. She described him living with her and how difficult that was—he'd lie around all day, not get up for work, lose his job, rely on her to care of the home and get groceries, and generally not contribute or pull his weight. She concluded that the best solution was for him to live elsewhere, since watching this behaviour was wearing her down, and her solution was to buy him an apartment or condo.

Bingo! We felt like we were in a similar situation with Ben. We didn't want to live with him but we didn't like where or how he lived when he wasn't at home. We needed to get him a living situation we were comfortable with so we could relax and get on with our lives! As the other mother continued talking, I pictured a lovely one-bedroom condo, clean, with granite countertops and a small living area. It sounded brilliant to me. I wasn't sure we could afford that solution for Ben—but then I had a fantastic idea.

What if we could connect these two boys and they could live together? They could support each other in their efforts to get and stay well. They could have a healthy, safe place to live that wasn't under their parents' roof, which would prevent them interfering with our well-being. They'd be independent in their day-to-day lives. They'd get a boost from us until they could get into the swing of this sober-adult-life thing. And we could split the costs! It was a perfect solution, I thought. All of this passed through my head in a matter of about 10 minutes, as others in the room shared. I got increasingly excited as I thought more and more about it. I impatiently sat through the rest of the meeting, not listening to anything anymore. I was so anxious to speak with her.

The meeting ended, and I raced over to talk with her as she was putting on her coat. Over the noise of people stacking chairs, I told her I related to her story. I said I admired her solution of finding her son a place to live. I shared with her that I had the same dilemma with my own son—our struggles were similar. The words poured out of me as I described similar feelings. I said my son was 18 years old. How old was her boy?

"He's 45 years old," she said.

I was struck dumb.

I was nearly 45. It was like a slap in the face to hear that the mother of a 45-year-old was experiencing the same problems I was. "Oh, my God," I thought. "I'm not willing to be still trying to solve this problem 27 years from now but that's what'll happen if I don't make a change."

It was a moment of grace. I had to figure out another way to behave or I'd wind up like her, sitting at a meeting like this one, talking about cashing in retirement savings to support my middle-aged son. It seemed utterly unacceptable to me that a 45-year-old man would be relying on his mother in this way, and yet, here I was willing to do the same for an 18-year-old. It was crystal clear to me in an instant; it was up to me to change or nothing would change.

This, more than anything, inspired me to start thinking about my boundaries. I began to consider them in terms of what I was willing to do beyond merely setting rules. Today, I understand boundaries as something we put around ourselves, for our own sakes. Something to which you apply the words, "I will." *Rules* are something you impose on another person. Something to which you apply the words, "You won't."

My previous understanding of boundaries had more to do with being clear about rules and conditions for our adult kids living with us. And my secret hope was that we would put those boundaries in place and in turn, they'd influence our kids to comply with our rules.

The line between boundaries and rules are blurry. Boundaries in the recovery community were initially presented as "tough love"—an approach that seemed meant to drive people toward sobriety by their friends and families refusing to support them if they used drugs and alcohol. This concept overlapped with the notion of "raising the bottom" by allowing the negative consequences of using that nudged users toward their "bottoms" sooner in the interest of having them choose sobriety sooner. It made some sense at the time, and we worked hard to be consistent in providing support to Ben if he was willing to exhibit healthy behaviours while refusing to support him if he wouldn't.

For teens, "raising the bottom" may mean mandating treatment, and for adults this may mean letting them handle their own debt, tickets, lost employment, or legal repercussions. I don't subscribe to saving them their pain by taking it on. And I don't subscribe to creating consequences purely for the sake of creating pain to motivate others to do what we want them to do.

My understanding of boundaries would evolve over the years to come, but for now, it was centered around the importance of consistency and what kind of support we were willing to engage in, based on possible outcomes. For example, we weren't willing to support Ben if he was using because using might lead to his death and we didn't want to have any role in supporting that outcome. Boundaries, in my mind, had to be something I was willing to enforce forever.

I began asking myself a question each time I considered doing something to "support" Ben: "Am I willing to be doing this for another 27 years?" With regard to paying his rent for an apartment (where, incidentally, he could potentially use drugs and alcohol), the answer was a resounding no. I wasn't willing to pay for his accommodations for the rest of his life, and I wasn't willing to have him live with us while using drugs or alcohol. That was clear. And I still hoped that he'd decide living sober with us was better than living in squalor and using.

We heard about "detachment with love" in Al-Anon as an ideal way to "be" with an addict. We knew it had something to do with boundaries but no one seemed able to clearly explain it or give us guidelines. Today, I describe detachment with love as caring about myself as much as I care about you. It's about ensuring there is enough distance between us so that I can be healthy while loving you.

In the year after Ben left Narconon, he returned to us four times. Each time Ben came to us asking to move home, asking for support, and saying he'd had enough of using, we'd get hopeful that this was the moment when it would all turn around. The first time this happened, I remember thinking, "*Yes*! Our boundary worked! He's now ready to make a change." I'd welcome him back and anxiously help him move, get his laundry clean, feed him, and happily step in and help organize his life. After a short time, Ben would relapse and we'd be back at square one, asking him to leave. And each time he returned, we got a little more jaded; we asked for more of a demonstration of his commitment to recovery and did a little less in terms of stepping in to organize and manage him. We were detaching but it felt like it was more out of discouragement than maintaining a healthy distance. What was this "detachment with love" we kept hearing about in Al-Anon? How did it look and feel, and how did you achieve it?

By August, we felt like we were in a holding pattern with both Ben and Ally. Ally was still cutting, but we were taking all the advice we could get in seeking help for her. Ben was living on his own and using once again. But at least Sam and Sydney were doing well. Things felt relatively stable, and we were sort of limping along. We thought we'd seen the worst of it. We thought things could only get better but we had no idea what was coming.

Reflective Questions:
- How are you "managing" your loved one?
- What lengths are you going to in order to set them up for success?
- Do you see yourself and your patterns in the story you just read? What are the similarities? What are the differences?

CHAPTER TEN

It was the spring of 2012 and Sam was 20 years old. He had just finished his first two years of engineering school, and he was home from university for the summer. His scholastic gifts seemed to be assuring him of a bright future and his childhood focus on engineering was still going strong.

He and Ben had partied through middle and high school, and while Ben's lack of focus and ambition had worried us, Sam's ambition and focus was always reassuring. I believed he was a lot like his dad and me, determined to have fun and at times careless and reckless but when it was time to be responsible and start a career, he'd sober up, get serious, and get on with life. When he joined a fraternity at university, I thought, "He was born for this." I was only slightly startled at Sam's description of the hazing and his admission of drug use, namely marijuana, in the fraternity house. Again, he seemed to be handling it all well enough and truth be told, I was incredibly proud of him.

Sam continued to party when he came home from university. He went out many weeknights, sometimes overnight, and sometimes he came home in the wee hours. I hated the influence that he might be having on Ben, even though Ben was living out of the home at the time. Sam worked hard at his landscaping job during the day and came home exhausted, only to rally after a quick shower and head out with friends, including Ben. Given our two-year struggle with Ben's addictions, I was disappointed and frustrated that they were partying together. Sam argued that Ben wasn't an addict, or even if he was, Sam wasn't willing to regulate or monitor him. Ben could come and party if he chose to; Sam wasn't willing to interfere.

One day toward the end of August, while I was in a meeting at work, my phone began ringing. I could see on the display that it was my husband and when he called for the third time in an hour, I stepped out to answer. Sounding scared and confused, Steve said Sam had left some strange messages, such as "I cannot believe you would betray me like this" on Steve's voicemail, and now wouldn't answer his phone. I leaned into the meeting room and excused myself for the rest of the day. I quickly packed my things, determined to find Sam, and get to the bottom of what was happening.

I arrived at the landscaping company to ask if Sam was there, only to find a young man who seemed a little nervous. He told me Sam had had an argument with his supervisor and stormed off on foot. This was out of character. I dialed his number. There was no answer. I redialed. No answer. I drove around looking for him, searching various routes between his employer and our home but there was no sign of him. I called Steve and Ben. Ben said Sam had answered one of his calls but wouldn't speak and then hung up. I had goosebumps as I listened to this account of Sam's behaviour. It was so unusual for him.

I headed home. Steve called and said he made it through to Sam's cell phone but it wasn't him who answered, rather someone who said he'd found Sam's cell phone and backpack on the tracks of Calgary's light rail system, the C-Train.

I felt like I was thinking and moving in slow motion. It dawned on me that I needed to call the police and get some help. I picked up our home phone and looked up the nonemergency number to report Sam missing. As my girls sat in the kitchen listening, I spoke with an officer and began answering questions about Sam. I responded to questions about his history, saying that he'd never had a history of mental health issues, aside from a strange incident earlier in the week.

A few days prior, I'd found a barely legible note from Sam on the passenger seat of my car that seemed to be to saying "Goodbye." That morning, I'd gone out to the garage and hopped into my car, annoyed to find the driver's seat reclined. I paused momentarily wondering why on Earth the seat would be laid back. I got in, put the seat up, and noticed a piece of paper on the passenger seat. I picked it up and struggled to decipher the writing. It appeared to be a note of apology from Sam and alluded to his ending his life. It was hard to see the words and they didn't make a ton of sense. But I was alarmed and went back in the house to show the note to Steve. We woke Sam up and asked him about it. I couldn't seem to rid my voice of irritation at the delay to my workday, despite my internal worry that this could be serious. Sam reassured us that it was nothing to worry about; he was drunk the night before and was "just messing around." We believed him enough that we both headed to work.

As I recounted this story to the police, I thought about how things must've looked and sounded to my girls, still sitting near me in the kitchen listening to every word. I didn't want to worry them but I knew I had to answer the questions honestly.

While I was speaking to the police on our landline, my cell phone rang. I asked the officer to hold on a moment—I hoped it was Sam. I answered and it was the police! I thought, "Wow, that was quick." I figured someone had already found Sam—even before the report was complete! I was impressed.

But that's not what had happened. While I was on the phone, Sam had walked into a different police detachment and offered himself up for arrest.

I let the first officer know that Sam had been found and ended the call. I returned to my cell phone and the female constable on the other end let me know that Sam was safe, was with her, and could use my support. I wasn't sure what that meant. I hung up and quickly jumped in my car, driving the endless 20 minutes to the police station. When I got there, the constable met me in the lobby. In a very calm and measured tone, she told me what had happened to Sam over the last hour.

She said he'd wandered into the station with his hands in the air saying he was turning himself in for terrorism. They interviewed him and he said he knew they were looking for him and was ready to turn himself in. There was no indication from the constable that they believed he was a terrorist. Instead, they asked if he had a history of mental health issues. They wanted to know what he'd been doing over the past few days.

I entered the tiny interview room where Sam was sitting and immediately noticed his dilated pupils. He appeared tense. His eyes darted between me and the constable, studying us both. He wasn't his usual logical and clear-thinking self. His speech was disjointed but he seemed to be considering his words carefully. The constable left the room, and I sat and spoke with him. I asked him what had happened at work and during the time he was missing. His account of the day was choppy and included irrational and unfounded statements about us reporting him to authorities and about people following him.

Sam was paranoid. I found myself speaking with him as though he were a psychiatric patient who might have presented to me in the emergency department years and years prior. I spoke slowly, calmly, and rationally, even though inside, I felt neither calm nor rational.

I excused myself from the room to speak privately to the constable. I said I'd never seen him like this before, that he had no psychiatric history, and that we needed help. I wasn't comfortable with the idea of putting him in the car and taking him home. I was in way over my head. Sam needed serious help. The constable agreed, and she and her partner placed Sam in the back of a police car to take him to the hospital while I called Steve and prepared to follow.

I was moving on autopilot. Just before we left the police station, I asked the officers what they thought could be going on and what might happen next. One of them said Sam seemed like someone with schizophrenia. I struggled to bring to mind the characteristics of schizophrenia, recalling vaguely that it was characterized by delusions and disordered thinking. I tried to absorb this information on the drive to the hospital but try as I might, I just couldn't understand how that word could have anything to do with me or my family. It just wasn't sinking in.

I felt like I was watching everything unfold on a screen, rather than living the experience myself.

That evening, Steve and I sat in the hospital's emergency waiting area for hours. We could hear Sam's raised voice behind the triage desk, hollering things that didn't make any sense. It was terribly upsetting. We waited for the nurses and doctors to assess him and determine the next step. What was causing all this?

In the meantime, I couldn't even make simple decisions. Was I hungry? Did I want something to eat? I couldn't remember when I'd last eaten. When we got up to walk to a vending machine, my legs felt like cement, like the force of gravity had somehow increased exponentially; it was too difficult to fight it and stay on my feet. I wanted to lie down in the hallway and sleep.

Sam was admitted to the psychiatric floor, and doctors informed us he was either showing the first signs of schizophrenia, which tends to show itself around the early twenties, or he was experiencing drug-induced psychosis. We wouldn't know which was the cause of his psychosis for about a year, the length of time he needed to be drug-free before we could attribute anything to a psychiatric disorder. He'd disclosed to doctors that he used a lot of drugs, mostly marijuana and occasionally prescription medication for ADHD if he needed to study before tests, while at university.

Marijuana was prolific at the fraternity house and Sam had smoked a lot of it. He had started experimenting as a young teen and his use increased drastically while away at school. The doctors told us marijuana was anything but harmless, especially on the developing brain. His state could've been caused by the drugs but they wouldn't know for sure until he stopped using for an extended period of time. In the meantime, Sam was seriously ill. He was suffering a psychotic break, which was an acute brain injury in which he experienced a reality that wasn't real. He needed rest and conversations with his family to gently reorient him.

Steve and I had previously booked a trip to visit my brother and his family, as well as old friends in Ontario, and Sam's sudden hospitalization had us discussing what to do next. I wasn't functioning well. I had trouble managing my emotions—crying, then getting angry, and then numb. Steve kindly agreed to stay home and manage things while I went to visit friends and family with the girls. The girls helped me pack and off we went for a week of respite.

Of course, it was anything but respite. I didn't feel like myself and had trouble focusing on the people I was there to see. Sam, and our family's crisis, lurked beneath every interaction, every activity.

The plan was to discharge Sam once he stabilized after a week or two and send him home on antipsychotics. He'd then follow-up with a psychiatrist for at least a year. His physician recommended that he take a semester off school at the minimum to give him some rest and reduce stress on his already stressed brain.

Sam came home after a couple of weeks in the psych unit, fragile and sedated.

All the chaos made work seem more difficult. Throughout that summer and fall, there was turmoil in one of the clinics I managed. I slept poorly, felt chronically stressed and dissatisfied with my job, and struggled to cope. My mind was a hamster wheel and my sense of self was crumbling as things around me at work and home fell apart. I took a couple of weeks off in September to try and regroup.

I'd always felt like a person who could "power through" issues, and this new feeling of not being able to function or function well was hard to accept. It was tough to admit I needed time off and even tougher to ask for it. Then came a manager meeting during which my anger brought me very close to saying something that would've had permanent consequences, and I suddenly realized that I really needed to stop, slow down, and take some time to look after myself. Then maybe I could at least curb these mounting feelings of recklessness and give proper attention to my struggle to control some destructive impulses. I walked out of that meeting and went straight to my doctor's office. He recommended a couple of weeks off and advised me to look after myself.

For me, looking after myself had always been about managing things around me. I really didn't know what it could mean beyond my traditional "self-care" strategies, which included massages or hair and nail appointments.

After a couple of weeks of sleeping in, reading, and spending quite a bit of time trying to relax, Steve and I talked and I made the decision to leave my job in the new year. I'd graduated with my master's from a leadership program a year prior and thought I could make the leap from health care management to consultant. Maybe being self-employed would help—I could set my own hours, regain a sense of influence as an external leadership consultant, and be home more to support the family. At the end of November, I gave notice at work—I'd leave at the end of February 2013.

Sam did take the semester off and he did follow up with his new psychiatrist, who specialized in psychosis and schizophrenia, and he did take his medication. What he didn't do was follow the recommendation that he get onto a regular schedule and stay off drugs or alcohol. He was susceptible to psychosis and ran the risk of another psychotic break, one from which he might not fully recover. And still, he kept somewhat irregular hours and continued to use.

I didn't understand how he could take the risk. Why wasn't he doing what the doctors recommended? Didn't he want to feel better? Didn't he want to go back to school and the life he'd been pursuing? Was his lifelong goal of being an engineer not enough to motivate him to get healthy and back on track?

It was a tough autumn, watching Sam defy doctors' orders and become increasingly numb and sedentary on antipsychotics. He sat on the sofa most days, not doing anything, and then stayed up late into the night, sometimes all night. We found beer cans in the basement so we knew he was drinking and he would admit to pot use if we asked. I remember having discussions with him, saying things like, "Sam, you need to make looking after yourself a priority." He responded with frustration, saying the things he needed to do to be "healthy" were boring. He felt that his lack of self-care was his own problem and asked why I cared so much. He insisted he was the only person truly affected and if he chose behaviours that ultimately left him feeling unwell, he should be allowed to.

How could he be so blind? While I understood his resistance to the tedium of looking after himself—of eating regular meals, sleeping regular hours, and getting regular exercise—why couldn't he see that his health and his struggles had an effect on all of us?

Meanwhile, Ben had been supportive of all of us during Sam's illness and he expressed a desire to sober up and live at home again. We'd been on the rollercoaster of his coming and going for over a year, and each time he showed up at our door vowing he was ready to change, we put less and less stock in what he said. His words had begun to feel hollow. Perhaps, this shake-up in our family had been the wake-up call he needed to finally get and stay sober. So in the late fall of 2012, he moved home.

We once again had a houseful of kids and sincerely hoped that, with support, they could move toward learning how to look after themselves and committing to it too. By December, against his doctors and our advice, Sam decided he felt well enough to go back to school for the rest of the semester. I had mixed feelings. I was worried that he was heading back to a stressful, toxic, and drug-ridden environment in a vulnerable state, even though he had found a new place to live off-campus. He was not recovered. He seemed fragile. And at the same time that I felt concern for him, I also felt some relief—our home might feel more peaceful with him gone.

As you might imagine, this experience led me to a lot of reflection and reading about marijuana and below you'll find some of my key takeaway points.

- No drug is harmless.
- According to research,[5] drugs, including marijuana, affect the brain and can cause psychosis.
- According to research, the teenage brain is particularly susceptible to the adverse effects because it's still in a developmental phase. Not everyone who uses marijuana as a teen develops psychosis but it dramatically increases the risk of psychosis, which can be permanent.[6]

Endnotes

5   https://www.drugabuse.gov/publications/research-reports/marijuana/there-link-between-marijuana-use-psychiatric-disorders,

https://americanaddictioncenters.org/marijuana-rehab/effects-of-marijuana-on-teenage-brain,

https://www.procon.org/files/current_psychiatry_psychosis.pdf

6   https://www.drugabuse.gov/publications/research-reports/marijuana/there-link-between-marijuana-use-psychiatric-disorders,

https://americanaddictioncenters.org/marijuana-rehab/effects-of-marijuana-on-teenage-brain,

https://www.procon.org/files/current_psychiatry_psychosis.pdf

CHAPTER ELEVEN

As planned, I left my job in health care at the end of February 2013. I was excited about a three-week trip to Europe that Steve and I had planned. A friend had suggested that we do it when I made the decision to leave my job and we loved the idea. We reasoned that it would be harder to find time later, since I didn't know how much time I would have once I became self-employed, and this could be a great way to mark the transition from employee to entrepreneur.

Our excitement was somewhat dampened by our worry about leaving the kids. Things were still chaotic. Sam was struggling to cope at university and was phoning us regularly in crisis over the simplest of problems. Ally continued to self-harm despite regular appointments we had in an adolescent mental health program. And Ben was once again on a downward trajectory with his drug use and old behaviours of partying, sleeping in, and lying. Syd was still flying under the radar, spending most of her spare time in her room. She seemed indifferent to us going.

But there was no end in sight, and we were beginning to accept that the issues our kids were experiencing were long-term. We concluded that it may never be a "good time" to get away and that this was probably as good a time as any, so we went.

We let Ben know he couldn't live in our home while we were away, and we hired a university student who'd worked for me as a clerk to stay in our home with Sydney and Ally. Ben agreed to leave without a fuss and moved out the day before we left.

Steve and I had a fantastic three weeks away, worrying relatively little and focusing on ourselves and each other. It was a great trip but by the end of the three weeks we felt ready to come home. We missed the kids!

When we returned, we discovered that for at least two of the three weeks we'd been gone, Ben had slept on park benches. It had been cold in Calgary, even snowing many of those nights. I felt awful when I learned this.

Steve and I had been living a dream while our son shivered through long dark nights in the snow. He said he had to get up every hour or so and move around to keep warm. How had I failed to notice that he didn't move to another home? It's possible that he had told me that he'd be staying with a friend. I'd been busy with planning for the girls and packing. What kind of a mother failed to notice where her son was going? How had I been so willfully blind?

I'd noticed that fatigue and a sense of hopelessness settled over me when it came to Ben. We'd been through so many ups and downs with him and my hopes had begun to harden. I realized I no longer wanted to hear his declarations or promises to change. I'd stopped believing him. The words weren't only hollow in my ears, they also felt like tiny paper cuts, aggravating and painful, little reminders of all the broken promises we'd heard before.

Then shortly after we arrived home in April, Ally confided to the visiting psychiatrist at the mental health clinic that she occasionally felt like people were watching her or calling her from behind when she was out for a walk. She would turn around but no one would be there. Auditory hallucinations were added to her list of symptoms, and we were referred to the same psychiatrist Sam had been seeing, who mercifully recognized our last name and fit us in rather quickly so we didn't have to wait the standard eight months for an initial consult. The psychosis that Sam had had, and the auditory hallucinations that Ally had, were both on the list of potential symptoms of schizophrenia but that was it. Neither of them was experiencing enough symptoms to be considered schizophrenic. Ally began taking antipsychotics, and we started the tedious process of finding one that managed her symptoms without horrible side effects. So at this point, we had two children who were experiencing psychotic symptoms with unknown causes and cures.

By the end of April 2013, Sam was home again from university and saying he was struggling to find hope or meaning. School had been overwhelming, and he'd failed many of his courses. He could no longer see a future for himself. He resigned himself to do a series of jobs that summer, struggling to stay employed. Ally was finishing up grade 10 and missing some classes because of stress, and Sydney was completing grade 11 in her customary quiet and undemanding manner. Ben had found a place to live and was doing some landscaping once again. Steve was travelling a great deal for work, and I was working from home, sitting in my tiny bedroom office and trying to focus on what exactly I was offering with my new business.

When I had occasion to pass through the living room, I saw Sam on the sofa, aimless, sedated, and playing games on his laptop. I struggled to retain a sense that we were on the right track. He looked miserable.

One day as I was struggling to work through a project in my home office, he came in, plopped down in the chair facing my desk, and sighed loudly. He said that he "just couldn't see the point" and that he was feeling hopeless about his future. He did this about once a week despite the medications and the regular visits with his psychiatrist. On this particular day, my pep talk and solution du jour was that he'd benefit from exercise. I convinced him, and myself, that coming to the gym with me was a step in the right direction. We were feeling positive and optimistic. Off we went to work out together. Sam seemed to feel a little better and so did I. Were we on to something? We went to the gym a few more times but before long Sam decided it wasn't working and resumed sitting on the sofa with his laptop.

This scenario of him feeling hopeless and coming to me, and me responding as though I could fix it with a conversation or a plan to stay busy and make healthy choices, would play out again and again, and I vividly remember the day I thought I'd reached a breakthrough. I helped Sam do a values exercise in which you take a stack of cards with values written on them and choose the ones that mattered most to you. Surely that would provide clarity and direction on what mattered! I handed him my deck of values cards and instructed him to pick out his top ten values, then scrap five of them, and then place the remaining five in order of importance. It was a well-meaning diversion for a few hours but useless in dealing with the very serious mental health issues he was trying to handle. Each time I'd come up with a new "solution" for Sam, Ben, or Ally, I'd get a little hopeful but I'd always end up devastated when the positive effects didn't last.

If I felt this way, I can't imagine how hopeless and desperate my kids felt.

Each time Ally or Sam had an appointment with the psychiatrist, I was required to attend for a few minutes to offer my account on how they were doing—their mood and behaviours. I found this exceedingly tough. I would join them briefly, and each time I'd think, perhaps this was my chance to have a say and maybe get a handle on where we were headed. I wanted to feel more like a collaborator in their plan of care and feel valued by "the system" for the effort and role I played in working toward supporting their recoveries.

Further, I wanted to be told that the hopelessness and chaos we were experiencing with our kids could and would improve. I wanted hope. I wanted some recognition that Steve and I were trying our best and doing as well as anyone could be expected to do. I wanted so badly to be seen and validated as a good mother who was working tirelessly to support her kids and know that eventually everything would have a positive impact.

But at each appointment, I felt peripheral at best and invisible as a person who *also* needed to be heard and supported. I felt incidental, like my utility as a caregiver was restricted to providing input on how the kids seemed to be doing. I began to suspect that perhaps my desire to be heard and seen was a sign of weakness and that prevented me from seeking help for myself. I believed that a stronger person would've been able to manage her own needs and be content to allow the focus to remain on the "patient." I made efforts to behave this way, to ignore what I wanted and needed, and I redoubled my efforts to appear like I had it together as a strong and supportive mother.

I wish I had asked for more help for myself but I clung to the notion that my own needs somehow meant that I was not good at helping and supporting the "real" patients. But caregivers need support. I recommend that if you're caring for another person, you seek care for yourself as well. I suggest you find a counsellor of your own in addition to taking some time with your loved one's caregiver. If this is new to you and you're not sure how to even start the conversation, you could begin by speaking to your loved one's counsellor about it.

Here are some statements you might use to ask for what you need:

"I would like to have some time to talk with you about how this has been for me. Is there time that we could do that?"

"I am interested in seeking support for myself so that I can continue to support my loved one. Could you recommend someone?"

"Being the primary support for my loved one can be exhausting at times. I need to find someone to talk to about how to best care for myself in this journey. I would love a referral or recommendation if this is not something you can provide."

Make those statements your own and find any courage you can to advocate for yourself. You'll be a better support to others if you do.

CHAPTER TWELVE

It had been a long spate of appointments, driving across the city in rush hour, and juggling work and sports for the girls with meetings and interventions for the boys. One rainy day in May, Ally and I were at her psychiatrist's office and I was once again called in to offer insight on how she was doing. During this appointment, her doctor had heard something from Ally that seemed to explain why our months of messing around with various antipsychotics hadn't had any effect and provided a clue to another potential diagnosis. She quickly turned, pulled out a heavy book that looked dense with text, opened it, and set it on her desk. She slid it in front of Ally and asked her to read a list of symptoms. From where I sat, I couldn't clearly see the writing on the page. Ally read the list of symptoms on the page and nodded, saying, "Oh yeah, that's me."

Her psychiatrist explained that Ally was reading from the Diagnostic and Statistical Manual—the bible of psychiatric disorders—and had identified with a qualifying five of nine symptoms associated with borderline personality disorder (BPD). She further explained that at 15, Ally wasn't old enough to be officially diagnosed with a personality disorder (personalities aren't fully formed until a person is 18) but she certainly fit the profile of someone with BPD.

I began to cry.

I had no idea what BPD was, but it didn't sound good and I couldn't seem to stop crying long enough to ask questions. Ally's doctor continued to talk about strategies for treatment. I continued to cry silently and didn't absorb anything she said. Eventually, her doctor acknowledged my tears by saying, "Mrs. Towns, I can see you're struggling. I can suggest some books for you to read that will explain the disorder." But I didn't want a book. I didn't feel like I had it in me to go home and begin "researching" a new problem. Although a diagnosis could've led us to treatment that might've been more helpful than the path we'd been on for the past year and a half, I felt like there would be no end to the disorders and problems in our home. Borderline personality disorder…what fresh hell was this? It had been two years of crisis after crisis by this time.

I numbly went home, talked with Steve, and looked into the treatment Ally's doctor had suggested, DBT, or dialectic behavioural therapy. We registered Ally for the 16-week skills program, although, I was cautioned, it could be years before she was healthy so I shouldn't put too much stock in the 16-week timeline. I was concerned about the expense; how would we find the money? We had already used a line of credit and credit cards to pay for Ben's interventions and treatments. But we didn't have a choice. Ally needed help. We reined in our fears and resolved to move ahead with treatment.

DBT is the gold standard of care for BPD. It's a form of behavioural therapy designed to help with emotional regulation, and we were advised to seek treatment with a company called Inner Solutions who, we were told, delivered the therapy to an unusually high standard. By that, I mean they didn't promote a DBT-informed therapy that only incorporated a few skills into their treatment. They weren't providing skills to a group and then letting people practice without support. They were a group that made themselves available to teach the skills and then they offered trained psychologists available via text for when a client experienced a disruption in thinking or mood. Clients could obtain support from their therapists in the moment they were struggling, which was when practicing the skills was toughest. This was the intent of the therapy when it was developed by Dr. Marsha Linehan.

Learning about DBT and more about BPD helped me to understand more about Ally and her cutting. I learned that self-harm is an attempt to control, isolate, and numb unpleasant feelings. It's a refocusing technique. My understanding is that Ally experienced strong and overwhelming emotions and she didn't know how to process them. By cutting, she could take control of where and what she felt. She'd feel emotionally numb by causing herself physical pain, effectively overriding the sensation pathway in a manner she could control. Where Sam and Ben used substances to escape their emotions or to stimulate more desirable feelings, Ally used cutting.

I went to the weekly mandatory mother-daughter information sessions for a few weeks, feeling angry. I was not myself. Today, I would be grateful for the education. But at this point, I was exasperated at this requirement. I thought I had enough on my plate without playing mindfulness games with other mothers and daughters. I just wanted Ally treated; I didn't want to be treated myself, and I certainly didn't feel like being educated on skills that were Ally's to learn. I resented my time being taken up in this way because I was barely holding it together myself and felt that there were better ways for me to spend my hours and energy. I wasn't a pleasant participant in that class. I made an exaggerated show of effort each time we were asked to do something. But we got through it and Ally went on with her therapy.

Sam's hopelessness and desperation hit a peak toward the end of June, right about the time of the 2013 Calgary flood, and he was talking about wanting to die. This was alarming, to say the least, and he agreed to be taken to an emergency department for assessment. He was admitted to a psychiatric unit. As Canada Day, July 1, approached, I felt compelled to arrange a family celebration. Family celebrations had been important to us, and Steve and I worked hard to make things fun when everyone was together but that became increasingly hard as life went sideways with the kids. Still, we didn't let our very abnormal situation get in the way of trying to make things feel normal. Sam loved Monopoly so the plan was to head to the hospital as a family with snacks in tow and play a game of Monopoly.

It was bizarre, at best. We crowded around a table in the common area, sat on chairs stained with God knows what, and tried to ignore the institutional setting. Sam was sedated with antipsychotics, antidepressants, and the residual effects of sleeping meds. He sat with bandaged wrists because he'd tried to cut himself with a plastic knife the night before. We were regularly interrupted by other patients, one of whom carried the distinct odour of urine, and by the nurses, who were doing their 30-minute safety checks. I felt increasingly sad, increasingly agitated, and irritable as the day wore on but I continued to try to stuff it all down and pretend this was a "fun family day."

The whole city seemed to be rallying to help with flood cleanup efforts, and that evening Ally came to our room and excitedly asked for permission to pitch in with friends we'd never met, two boys she'd been chatting with on her phone. I was concerned, not only about the prospect of her heading off with strangers, but also about some of the risks associated with flood cleanup. Bacteria multiplies in stagnant water and water-damaged homes are a hotspot for potentially harmful mould. Protective gear was recommended for all people helping with the cleanup. We didn't have what she needed and we couldn't go with her so we told her she had to stay home. She was visibly deflated, despite our reasoning.

"Here we go," I thought. "She's going to do something stupid." Minutes later, I went to her room, gave a cursory knock, and opened the door. I was horrified. There she was, razor in hand, cutting her forearm. I feel nauseous just recalling how raw her arm looked. There sat my little girl on the edge of her bed, open wounds sliced into her arm. Her forearm looked like hamburger, and blood was dripping thickly and clotting on a Kleenex.

I didn't react well. I'm not proud to admit that I snapped at her. I told her abruptly to clean herself up. I took the razor away.

I feel such sadness as I reflect back on that experience. I didn't have the capacity or knowledge to give her what she needed. Instead, all my frustration with not knowing how to help my kids manifested in my short, clipped reprimand. This is among one of my saddest memories at failing to handle my kids' mental health issues and my regret at not having the skills to be the mother I wanted to be.

I'm confident today that if I'd been better at looking after myself and staying healthy, I would've been more centred in that moment. If I had sought my own therapy to assist me in learning how to feel my emotions as opposed to taking action to avoid feeling them, I would've been more capable of making myself present to her. Perhaps, if I'd been looking after myself, I would've accepted my feelings of sadness, fear, frustration, and pain, and I would've then been able to accept and validate Ally's struggle and tell her it hurt to see her hurt. I would have been able to tell her I love her, hug her, and sit with her and listen if she wanted to talk until she felt a little better. I would've been able to tuck her in and tell her I'd always love her and be with her when she needed me.

Eventually, I'd get to this place but not that night in July 2013.

On that night, I was still struggling with, and rejecting the idea that I had needs too. I was running on empty, and somewhere in my mind, I hoped that when everyone else became willing to embrace wellness, I would naturally feel better too. This was more of an assumption than a fully formed thought. The conscious thoughts were more like, "I have to keep fighting. I can't give up. If I keep trying, we'll come across something that will click for them and make them better." I just kept pushing my kids, pulling them, up, down, back, and forth, trying to find the "thing" that would get through and flick some kind of invisible switch.

About a week later, Sam was discharged home and referred to an out-patient program for patients with psychosis. He turned 21 at the end of the month, and we had his birthday celebration outside on the deck one warm summer evening. All the kids were there, and I sat watching them and reflecting.

Sam wasn't thriving by any stretch. His future was uncertain. He wasn't following through on recommended treatments, and he was a challenge to live with. He continued to use drugs and alcohol despite the serious risk of permanent brain damage with psychosis, not to mention the damage that it was causing to the atmosphere in our home. Somewhere in the back of my mind, a whisper started to make itself heard, saying that maybe he wouldn't stop using because he was an addict too.

Ben was also still struggling with drug use. He was living in another sketchy place a few neighbourhoods away. He didn't look well either, and I reflected that despite this, he'd made noticeable efforts to be supportive of Sam and us over the past year. By now, my fear for Ben was like a low, chronic hum. But that fear was mixed with gratitude and appreciation for his willingness to show up and be strong and calm, with genuine warmth, when those he loved were hurting. I was reminded of how big and generous his heart was.

And then, I looked at Ally. She'd withdrawn from me since my blow up at her a few weeks prior. She looked pale and unhappy despite her efforts to joke around with her siblings. Sydney also looked like she was trying to enjoy the family time despite the crazy year we'd had. I didn't know it at the time but she was really struggling too. I felt grateful to know that she was always in her room, safe and sound. She has told me since that she was anything but safe and sound. She was depressed, suicidal, and self-harming. She flew under our rather dull radar, feeling like her issues were not serious enough. So she stayed quiet and alone in her room most of the time, while we thought she was just getting away from the chaos. Not noticing Sydney's struggles is one of my other biggest regrets.

On this summer night, it felt bittersweet to have the family together. We so obviously loved each other and wanted to enjoy lighthearted family time. But looming over our heads were the issues we were trying to manage, like storm clouds on the horizon.

As we cleaned up dinner, I considered that soon we'd all be settling in for the night—all of us, that is, but Ben. I felt a little unsettled by this as I looked around the yard at my children. Ben had to leave and go back to his rented room in another part of the city, while the rest of the family could retire for the night cozy at home. It suddenly felt very wrong that Ben should have to leave us, and I recalled that same feeling I'd had when he was alone in Quebec for treatment while the rest of us were at home celebrating Christmas. It felt as if everyone else who lived there was struggling in some way despite the supports in place so why wouldn't we afford Ben the same support of living at home? Ben went home to his own place that night and it was hard to watch him leave. My heart ached.

Steve and I talked about the idea of changing our decision and inviting Ben back into our home. We were unsure—would we be enabling Ben by doing this? In the recovery community, the words "enabling" and "boundaries" come loaded with black and white thinking: Enabling is "bad." Anything that can be seen as permitting drug or alcohol use is also "bad." The idea of tough love, of kicking loved ones out of the house if they slip, is celebrated as the maintenance of firm boundaries. If you aren't willing to do that, you're soft and enabling. I'm not sure it *is* actually that black and white but as a person still relatively new to the concepts, that's how it seemed.

We decided that to be sure we weren't making a rash emotional move we'd come to regret (again), we'd consult with a trusted friend we knew from Al-Anon. We called Anne. She had a lot of experience with boundaries and having her kids move in and out of her home. We'd met her a year before. The three of us went for coffee, and she listened as we described our dilemma: We wanted Ben to live with us even though we knew he'd most likely continue to use drugs. "What's changed?" she quietly asked.

What changed was how we felt, and Anne said that was enough. She advised us that setting boundaries was about doing what we needed to get healthy and stay that way. If inviting Ben to live with us felt right, then it was. I remember her saying, "You get to do whatever you need to do so that you can sleep at night." If that meant doing something that could be considered enabling by more rigid standards, it was okay.

I loved this. It gave us freedom to make boundaries that worked not just for us but for our relationships with our kids. It felt like our boundaries were therefore part of self-care: "Anything that helps you sleep at night." It also allowed for our boundaries to shift over time. And it put the focus on our own mental and emotional health as opposed to Ben's behaviour. Boundaries weren't "tough love." Rather, it now seemed, they were about keeping yourself healthy and they included compassion for both yourself and the people around you.

Today, here's some of what I teach families who are struggling about boundaries:

- Boundaries are the physical, mental, and emotional dividing lines that set us apart from other people. We set them, or define them, to help us stay healthy. We can decide what is and isn't okay for us.
- A boundary is not a rule. A rule is meant to control or define another person's behaviour. A boundary honours the emotional and physical health of the person making the boundary.
- Boundaries can be physical, mental, emotional, material, and spiritual.
- Boundaries are individual and need to suit the person or people making them.
- Be patient. Learning boundaries is about taking steps toward health. You may not know what feels healthy immediately. That can take a while to figure out so don't rush.
- Even after you figure out what does and doesn't feel okay, learning to say "no" to others can be tough. Start small. Practice with a relatively inconsequential "no" before saying "no" to someone or some-

thing that may have more negative consequences (such as someone not liking you, being upset with you, or threatening to end a relationship). You may even start out by saying "no" to something and refraining to offer a reason when you normally would.

- It's okay if your boundaries change.
- Prepare for the fact that others may not like your boundaries.
- Making effective boundaries requires:
  - Acceptance of how you feel.
  - Acceptance of what's healthy for you.
  - The understanding that, ultimately, having and enforcing boundaries is an act of love and compassion.
  - The realization that having boundaries enhances and deepens your relationships in an authentic way (we develop and define boundaries in relationships that we want to last).
  - Knowing that effective boundaries allow you to be more loving and kinder to others.

CHAPTER THIRTEEN

By mid-August of 2013, we had all the kids under our roof again. We slept well at night with the feeling that we were back on track in supporting and helping them as best we could, despite the fact that they weren't thriving. This lasted about two months before the boys started keeping unpredictable schedules, using drugs, and leaving messes around the house again, and Steve and I felt we needed to make another change.

We began to consider if there were other types of support we could or should offer Ben. He really did seem stuck in his addiction, and I began to wonder if a different treatment centre could offer him a solid solution after all. I talked with a trusted friend I'd worked with in health care who knew a little of our story. Years ago, she had also supported her own teens through addiction and recovery. She described the program they went through and the high level of commitment that was expected of the entire family. She mentioned how opening up her home to the kids in the program and hosting them overnight while they were in treatment was part of the program. She said that those same sick kids who were unmanageable in their own homes helped out in her home, clearing the dishes, and saying, "Thank you."

"It was amazing to see the change in them," she told me. She talked about her daughter's recovery and the things that she personally learned through her involvement in the family-based program. She mentioned that her family had developed life-long friendships through the program. It all sounded like things I wanted for my family. She recommended that we explore the Alberta Adolescent Recovery Centre (AARC) for Ben. Initially, I suspected that Ben, now 20, was too old for the program, which focused on adolescents. But he wasn't! We consulted with AARC about Ben and also mentioned that we were wondering whether Sam might need the program.

AARC is a long-term adolescent treatment facility focused on the family. They specialize in treating kids between 12 and 21. Their program is based on the doctoral research of Dr. Dean Vause, the founder and executive director of the program, and some of its unique characteristics include recovery homes, group and family therapy, and one-on-one counselling for clients, siblings, fathers, and mothers. Under the auspices of AARC programming, parents and siblings attend mandated weekly meetings in which alumni of the program can also participate.

On a warm October day, Steve and I sat in our car, parked across the road from the Centre just off a busy thoroughfare in Calgary, and looked at the large, white, brick building. It was clean, tidy, and unnoticeable unless you were looking for it. While we sat there, a young, healthy-looking boy with dark hair came out of an unmarked door with a large, full bag of garbage. He had a bounce in his step and appeared to be singing to himself while he took the bag to the garbage bin, threw it over the rim, and cheerfully disappeared back through the door he'd emerged from. Steve and I looked at each other and remarked that this was impressive. The boy looked nothing like the clients we'd seen in the treatment centre in Quebec and nothing like what we guessed an adolescent drug addict in treatment might look like.

Inside, we completed our consult and assessment with one of the clinical directors and were also invited to chat with one of the program's peer counsellors. The counsellors at AARC are all graduates of the program. They're further trained and supervised by the clinical directors in their work with clients. They share their personal experiences in addiction, which resonate with the clients and provide a positive role model of hope and support. They're an incredible and important part of what makes the program so successful.

We were told that Ben certainly sounded like he belonged in the program. We were advised to wait and see with Sam—if he did seem to qualify then we could offer him the program a little later.

What really impressed me at that visit is that we didn't feel like they were selling us on their service. The program was a little more expensive than Narconon had been but the saying "you get what you pay for" rang in my ears. In fact, as we sat in the boardroom with the peer counsellor and the clinical codirector, we felt like we were being given a fair warning that the program isn't for everyone. The codirector even used those words. He was very forthright about the intense commitment required by the entire family, and he offered other resources we could access if we felt like we weren't ready for what AARC required. We were also given a multiple-page list of previous graduates and encouraged to call any of them to discuss their experiences.

This was very, very different from what we'd experienced with the centre in Quebec. After some deliberation, checking AARC's references and asking our other kids if they were willing to participate and thereby support Ben in treatment, we decided to offer the program to Ben. Once again, we sat down with him in our living room and talked about how things had been going with him at home. By now, the topic felt a little old, but this time, it really felt like we were offering hope. Rather than saying, "Do this or live without our support," we could honestly say "Here's our best support, we hope you take it." He accepted and agreed to be admitted at the end of the week.

Today, having had exposure to multiple treatment centres, multiple approaches to recovery, and many families with various experiences, I can claim a certain expertise when it comes to shopping for reputable programs. Here's what I recommend and wish I'd known back when we first began shopping for addictions treatment.

You and your family are your own best advocates in finding the right type of treatment and the best facility to provide it. Sometimes well-meaning health care professionals or other people in your life may point you in the wrong direction, simply because addiction treatment is not their area of expertise. It's enormously important that you slow down, take some time, and resist the urge to make decisions based on fear. You have to do your research. Get the names of treatment centres and call them. Ask about accreditation, research that supports their approach to treatment, and the level of education and experience of their staff. Don't be shy about asking any prospective providers a lot of questions and trust your instincts if you get answers that seem a little off the mark.

I recommend you start with a referral from someone who's walked the path before you—we are many. Anytime I've disclosed that I have kids in recovery, the person I've been talking with knows someone who knows someone who's been through it. Get referrals. Their advice will likely be better than anything Google brings up. Make a list of questions you'd like to ask and use the ones below as a guide.

- Can you easily find where the treatment centre is and gain access to a real person? You should be able to find the centre and talk with the people who provide treatment.
- What accreditation standards has the centre met, and how often does it meet them? Good programs will go through the process of accreditation.
- Does it have full-time staff providing a mix of individual and group counselling treatment? Do the staff have professional credentials as well as firsthand experience? In my experience, knowledge gained from only formal education is not enough. The ideal is a mix of personal experience and formal education.
- Is there someone in charge of your loved one's care, and do you have access for questions and updates? You ought to be able to get updates.
- Does the centre have experience in handling co-occurring disorders, like anxiety, ADHD, trauma, gambling, and BPD? Many, arguably all, addicted people have underlying issues that need addressing once they're sober.
- Does the centre or program have qualified professionals who can provide mental health assessments, identify appropriate interventions, and prescribe medications if required? As above, many addicts will need it.
- Is the program gender- and age-appropriate? Stronger treatment facilities will offer separate programming to address differences in age and gender.
- Does the program offer detox? Detoxification needs to be monitored by a qualified health professional.

- Does the centre have 24-hour medical care? Or on-call care? They should.
- Do the counsellors practice evidence-based treatments (or will they partner with organizations that offer them), such as:
  - Cognitive behavioural therapy
  - Dialectical behaviour therapy
  - Multidimensional family therapy
  - Medication-assisted treatment
- Does the centre readily provide their day-to-day schedule? A good centre will be transparent about the schedule of group and individual therapy sessions, recreational activities, chores, support groups, and a programming structure for both weekdays and weekends.
- Does the centre include family as part of the process? Does that process include treatment that addresses the family dynamic and complex and damaged relationships? Family education and treatment is critical.
- Does the centre have a very clear step-down—or discharge—process? A good program will offer transition support.
- Is there post-treatment support? Post-treatment support is important.
- Is the centre very clear and up front about costs? There should be no surprises.
- Does the centre have a policy of no kickbacks for referrals? No reputable centre will provide referral incentives.

CHAPTER FOURTEEN

AARC was as demanding as we'd been told to expect during the assessment. Our entire family was required to be on time and in attendance at all meetings unless otherwise excused by staff. Mandatory group therapy meetings were two evenings a week. Mandatory "parent cleaning days" were one Saturday morning each month: Parents gathered to clean and do minor repairs to the centre. There were two "parent days," all-day commitments twice a year in which we attended marathon group therapy sessions, in addition to all-day commitments on special occasions such as Christmas and Easter. There were other miscellaneous commitments as well, as directed by the centre. And we were committed to opening a recovery home to host kids in the program overnight and on weekends. The tremendous time commitment meant we pretty much couldn't have a social life outside the program.

On our first parent cleaning day—the second day for us at AARC—another parent further along in the program suggested that the best way to handle the commitments and the new culture of the program (which was full of hugs) was to "just drink the Kool-Aid." Steve replied that even if AARC did turn out to be a cult, he wouldn't care, as long as it worked.

I felt the same way. I remember thinking I would and could do anything they asked, as long as they took Ben and made him a functional and independent man. I'd been wondering and worrying about Ben for almost three years, and I felt like such a failure at raising and launching my kids. My hold on my identity as a strong woman who could do anything had been shaken to the core. I'd put a lot of energy into trying to appear calm and sane, and my hold on this facade was tenuous. I was exhausted.

We were told to expect Ben's attendance at AARC to last for the better part of a year. We were exposed to alumni as a community of support who could also sit in on our meetings and offer comments and insight if invited by the facilitator. This was a great way to get to know members of the recovery community who'd been through the same treatment, and they offered a sense of hope and focus in terms of what recovery for a parent or sibling can look like. This community would become increasingly important to me and my family.

I felt angry most of the time then but I was still afraid to appear that way, lest I be judged. And I was also afraid the counsellors at the treatment centre wouldn't be able to handle how angry I felt. I feared that if I let my anger seep out a little, it would shoot out of me in uncontrolled tongues of fire.

Family involvement in AARC was so intense that after about a month after Ben started, AARC agreed that Sam would also benefit from the program: They'd seen a lot of him during group therapy sessions, when the kids in treatment talked about their compulsions to use. The facilitator would jokingly ask the parents and siblings who among them could relate so as to underscore the contrast between an addicted person and a "normal" person. But more often than not, Sam *could* relate and he'd put up his hand. This, combined with insider knowledge of his using, likely from Ben's sharing, gave them enough to understand that Sam probably did belong there.

We decided to offer it to him—bearing witness every day to his apathy, lack of direction and self-care was becoming unbearable. We told Sam that we suspected he had an addiction issue and that he needed to move out or seek treatment. We advised him that we'd support his admission to AARC or that he could seek treatment somewhere else. We were nervous about making this rule for Sam. His moods were volatile; he seemed to slip into suicidality quickly and we worried about how he would handle what was, essentially, an ultimatum.

He responded calmly, but a day later he called me, waking me up at midnight, clearly upset and telling me he loved me and that he was calling just to say, "Thank you and goodbye." I was immediately on my feet. He told me that he was standing on the C-Train tracks downtown, crying with his cell phone in his hand, and I could hear the train horn as it raced toward him. With my phone in hand, I raced down the stairs and into my car, then drove up the highway. I dialed 911 from my car, hoping the police could get there in time to help him. The operator said she could see Sam on one of the city's cameras. She said the train had stopped and that the police were approaching to talk with him.

I parked where I had a vantage point of the police car and watched as the police escorted Sam across the lot. The officers called to tell me they were taking him to the hospital for assessment and likely an admission. I'd been in this position before and I knew what lay ahead for Sam. It was going to be a long night in the emergency department before admission to a psychiatric unit. I knew he'd be kept in a secure room where he couldn't hurt himself and I would have little access to him there. I let them drive away, turned my car around, and headed home. Steve was out of town working, and I called him from the car to fill him in on the events of the night. It was a tough call to make and, I'm sure, a tough call to get.

During his hospitalization, Sam disclosed more honestly how he'd been thinking and feeling. Apparently, he'd been guarded with his psychiatrist up to this point, which only interfered with his doctor's attempts to diagnose and treat him. Based on this new information, his psychiatrist referred Sam for some testing. He , too was diagnosed with BPD. Steve and I felt both relieved and surprised. This was the same diagnosis as Ally but he presented so differently than she did: Sam was defiant, addicted, and had attempted suicide, while Ally was self-harming. Getting him sober was a priority at this point. Less than a week later, he left the hospital and was admitted to AARC.

AARC was willing to work with the therapists at Inner Solutions so that Sam could take advantage of DBT (the same dialectical behaviour therapy prescribed to Ally) when he was ready and in combination with his treatment for addiction. Through consultation with AARC's psychiatrist, Sam's anti-psychotics were discontinued since they'd mentally and emotionally dulled him to the point that they would frustrate his participation in treatment.

I was finally forced to stop obsessing about how the boys were doing. For the first several months of the program, new clients are constantly supervised by staff and other, more senior clients; they're not permitted to spend time alone with family. The boys were being looked after and for the first time in years, I didn't need to think about how they were doing. This was a blessing but it was also a difficult transition. I was so accustomed to ignoring and avoiding my own feelings in favour of focusing on theirs. The chance to truly look after myself felt scary and unnatural.

Every Tuesday evening, we'd rush to AARC and sit under bright lights in the rows of folding chairs facing the front of the room, men on one side and women on the other. The newest people sat at the front and the more experienced sat toward the back. (You earned your seat at the back by working on your steps and supporting your child through theirs. The further along you were in treatment, the further you got from the front of the room, where the heavy lifting and focus generally was. New people needed the most time and attention from the clinical leaders so they sat closest to the front.)

Once everyone was settled, our group program, called Parent Rap, would begin. We'd talk about what our lives were like as the parents of sick kids. We'd discuss our struggles and our roles in the chaos that had become our homes. We volunteered to share by raising our hands and then we'd stand up and move to the wall at the front of the room to talk. Many people were shy with this method but I wasn't. From early days, I had my hand up. I had a lot to say.

One early December evening, I was on my feet and standing against the wall. I shared that I knew that the boys did chores during the day at AARC and that those chores would sometimes take them to the parking lot to sweep or take out the garbage. I told the group that I drove past the treatment centre during the day and craned my neck, stretching to look over the cement median at 70 km/hr to see if by chance I could spot my boys. I'd been missing them, worrying about them, and wondering how they were doing. Were they finding the program helpful? How were they feeling?

"You need to get a life," Natalie said. She was the clinical lead that evening and one of my favourites in the program. She said it gently, with some humour and with her characteristic directness.

We all chuckled a little but the message landed. I thought I was sharing my "motherly concern" for my boys but what she (very accurately) heard from me was this: Now that I had a chance to look after myself, I didn't know how. I had no clue what to do. So I continued to focus on the boys and spent my time looking for reassurance that they were doing okay, always looking for details about how they were feeling.

The first step to letting go of the boys and looking after myself was to make the decision to stop driving by the treatment centre looking for signs of them. I took Natalie's hint, trying to trust that they were fine and refocus my energy on myself. I was amazed at how much time and energy I'd previously spent on them. I began to notice each time they came to mind, and it happened a *lot*. It revealed to me that I'd let myself spend most of my mental and emotional time and energy on worrying and trying to manage them. (Ally had taken up my headspace as well but that had considerably diminished since she started DBT and had a regular therapist with whom she texted for support.)

In the absence of fear, which had fuelled me, I really started to feel tired—lie-down-in-the-street-and-sleep sort of tired. I started napping during the day, which felt decadent. And the longer it went on, the more difficult it was for me to accept. I was beat and I needed that sleep but it felt wrong somehow. And yet, once I got started, I couldn't seem to stop. I'd grow tired midday, find a quiet spot to lie down, and I'd be out like a light. I felt guilty for this—Steve was at work, the girls were at school, the boys were in treatment, and here I was napping! But boy, did I need that rest. I was worn down. I continued napping because it felt like my body wouldn't let me stop.

Winter arrived in Calgary full force, and on a cold Tuesday night in January, the theme at AARC was broken dreams. I was invited to share. I was in what I called my AARC uniform—a hoodie and track pants. I stood in front of the wall and began with, "I don't want the boys back after treatment. I just want them fixed and then you guys can help them find a place to live." And I meant it. I'd been feeling overwhelmed for years, and I had that unspoken expectation that if I loved them and kept them safe, they'd launch well in their early adult years and then I could enjoy them as people. More importantly, I could get on with having a life myself. When that didn't happen, I felt like a failure. I felt hopeless. I felt resentment. I'd done my part, done it to the best of my ability, and I'd failed. AARC could take it from there.

I made a lot of friends in AARC, and when some of the other mothers who were there that night talk about how I presented in early treatment, they tell me I looked and sounded sad and angry. I was unapproachable. I was hard as stone and tough to get through to. They said there were "waves of pain" coming from me as I shared how I felt. At that time, I didn't imagine ever having a healthy relationship with my boys. I was in salvage mode, determined to save myself. The counsellor working with me that evening advised me not to get ahead of myself, that I might feel differently when we completed the program, an estimated seven to nine months down the road. I desperately wanted to believe her, and I worried that while she may have seen this change in others, I'd be an exception. I worried that I was too far gone, too different than the other mothers, and I couldn't imagine my heart softening to the extent that I'd once again be happy to try parenting the children I'd already failed so miserably.

I've since learned that I was feeling "terminally unique." This term is used to describe the belief among struggling people that they're too special to be helped. We "terminally unique" believe no one can understand us, no one has ever been this messed up, and no one has ever seen what we've seen. No one can reckon with the depths of our pain. We think we're alone, special, and beyond the reach of those there to help. But really what we've done is come up with an excuse to stay a victim of our circumstances, to stay sick. This perspective gives us an "out" when things get difficult and things always get difficult when you're trying to get better. "What if I really am so different from anyone who has ever gotten better?" We say to ourselves. "That would mean that maybe feeling or getting better is beyond me." It's a mindset driven by the fear that this could actually be true. This illness prevents us from seeing choices and ensures we don't earnestly look for help. It keeps us distant and apart. It allows our fear to grow stronger.

As a mom, I'd always felt different. I wanted to be strong, but beyond that, I didn't know what I was striving for, aside from the ultimate outcome of well-adjusted kids. When I looked around me for clues as to what a mother was supposed to be, I didn't identify well with what I saw—not the traditional June Cleavers I saw on TV as a kid, nor the modern ideal that I was seeing in the current media and online. As my kids were growing up, the media portrayed the ideal as "yummy mummies" and MILFs. (Making sexual desirability a desirable trait for a maternal figure has always felt a little weird to me.)

At the schools my kids attended, I noticed many of the other mothers checking each other out and gossiping. They escorted their kids to school and then hit the gym. Many were vocal complainers about their children not being seen as the prodigies they knew them to be, and they'd brag about fighting for their children with anyone or anything that didn't support their view. They strove for the illusion of perfection, even right down to "fun, new, and visually appealing snack ideas." Meanwhile, online, mothers were getting famous making videos about "wine o'clock" and confiding their parenting foibles as evidence that they were, after all, fallible and fun.

I didn't have a close relationship with anyone I wanted to emulate as a mom. I didn't know who to model myself after or how to conceptualize who I wanted to be as a mom. My own mother was an enigma to me and my relationship with her was strained. I admired strong women and knew some that I liked but I wasn't sure who they were as mothers.

This motherhood issue came up for me again in treatment at AARC. A part of me wanted to fit in with the other moms and a part of me didn't. I seemed more quickly able to notice our differences than our similarities. And when I did notice a difference, I made it a bigger deal than it needed to be. This behaviour made me feel sad and lonely, even as I clung to it. Again, my terminal uniqueness was on full display.

My dedication to motherhood today is a commitment to being the mom my kids need me to be. When we started AARC, that commitment meant driving action, relentless forward progress, and fighting the good fight. Today, it means being compassionate and empathetic and making spending time with my kids a priority. It means being curious, inquisitive, supportive, and a cheerleader.

I believe my job is to be a role model of the pursuit of being wholly myself and true to my own nature and to show them that I support them in the pursuit of the same.

Reflective Questions:
- We all have beliefs about what it means to be a "good" wife, husband, father, mother, daughter, sister, etc. What beliefs are you

holding on to? What behaviours are they driving that keep you from "having a life?"

- What would it mean for you to let go of those old beliefs?
- What would be possible if you could shift those beliefs and focus more on looking after yourself?

CHAPTER FIFTEEN

I was a difficult person to help. I really gave people a hard time. I wanted to poke at them to see what they were made of before I let them in. I had some strong opinions (judgments) about who was capable and who was qualified to step into my world to give me a hand. For the most part, this was counterproductive; I'd seek help, then find a million and one reasons why a given person was incapable of actually doing me any good. I was arrogant and stubborn, and in early recovery, this would prove to get in my way. I had to become willing to let go and connect. I had to crack my hard shell open.

Additionally, I'd always been attracted to strong, direct, compassionate people who also seemed to be able to regulate their expression of emotion. By that, I mean I appreciated thoughts and emotions expressed honestly but in moderation, at the right time, and with the right people. I admired this, and I felt secure with people who practiced it. Passive people, the emotionally volatile, and those determined to please made me uneasy. I felt unsure around them, frustrated in our interactions; and I avoided them, feeling unsafe because they were unpredictable or because they were unreadable. I liked the honest transparency of assertive people.

Every parent was assigned a counsellor at AARC. We met one-on-one, about once a month. My first nurse counsellor at AARC was a little older than me. My initial impression of her was steeped in my own anger and, I later realized, very inaccurate. But back then, she seemed to exude kindness and an almost apologetic conservatism. Her voice was soft, her face kind and gentle. To my aggressive self, her gentleness seemed to verge on timidity. In group therapy, she offered statements that were intended to provide insight with softness that I read as bordering on the bashful. I was a person who showed up angry, exuding a don't-waste-my-time brusqueness, so her more subtle approach was lost on me.

We'd start our one-on-one sessions with a reading aloud from the AA Big Book and a prayer. I would sigh, close my eyes, and talk to myself during this time, saying things like, "Stay open, Maureen. This is not so bad. I know you don't agree with the words but the sentiment is harmless." Then she'd ask about my week. I'd respond with a story about an irritation I'd experienced, and she'd ask what I judged to be leading questions. I decided after only a couple of visits that she couldn't help me. She was soft, I thought, and I was tough. What had worked for her would in no way work for me.

So we got nowhere. I felt like we weren't digging deep enough or hard enough, and the more frustrated I got, the more nervous she seemed. When she left her position at AARC I was assigned to another counsellor, Joan.

Steve was seeing his own counsellor with whom he had a great rapport, and I found another mother to offer me additional one-on-one support through the program. This was recommended by staff, who'd given me her name thinking that she and I would be a good fit. The day of my first meeting with her, I was upset about something and wanted to vent about it so I let her know. Brenda appeared to be suppressing a smile as I held nothing back. I was swearing and somewhat sarcastic in my description of whatever situation I was relating. Even as she listened, it was clear to me that she wasn't falling for my version of the truth in whatever events I was describing. But as promised, she listened. She later told me that after that first meeting, she felt like I'd been trying to wrestle her for the imaginary reins of control. She felt as though I was challenging her a little to see if I could be "in charge" in our relationship. She said she walked away thinking, "This is an interesting woman" and that supporting me in my recovery would be a fun and interesting journey. Thank goodness there were people like her, willing to step into my combativeness to help me.

She'd been through a lot as a mom and understood that she'd be doing me a disservice if she was anything but firm and straightforward in her approach. She challenged me when I wasn't digging hard or deep enough, and I admired her for it. Deep down, I really wanted her approval. When we sat down to review how I reacted to my kids when they were using, I was nervous.

I hoped to "wow" her with my insight, but instead of telling me how impressed she was, she set an additional date to chat about some written work I had done for her, implying that I needed to do further exploration. One of the questions was, "What did you do when your efforts to manage your addict failed?" I wrote that I'd change tack. If I'd been firm and demanding, I'd try being soft and more collaborative. If I'd been compassionate and understanding, I'd try a more aggressive approach. Over a cup of coffee, sitting on Brenda's comfy sofa with a blanket on my lap, she asked me, "What do you think that was like for your family?"

I'd always felt very justified in my behaviours, believing that I was driven to them by circumstances. What else was I to do? At times, I felt a little out of control, but at other times, I felt rather clever, thinking that I was staying one step ahead of the boys. Until Brenda's pointed question, I'd never stopped to consider what the impact had been, especially for Steve and the girls. My ups and downs must have been palpable, unpredictable, and maybe even scary.

As I thought about that, tears welled up. How had I not considered this before? I must've been awful to live with and I began to see how I had contributed to the chaos in our home. My own father popped into my head and I quickly shrugged off the association. I felt so, so sad at this new awareness. I'd never intended to be difficult. I wondered, had my family been walking on eggshells around me?

Brenda reassured me, saying that if I was open to a different way of responding to my kids, there would be huge payoffs, not just for them but for me too. I remember her promising that if I opened up to pain, fear, and sadness, I'd also open up to a new level of joy, freedom, and appreciation for the beauty in the people and world around me—the greens would be greener and the blues would be bluer. She described the "AARC facelift," saying that if I did the work, others would notice a change not only in my attitude but also my appearance. She said that other parents seemed to physically change.

They became more attractive as their internal changes translated to the exuding of kindness and acceptance. I believed her and recommitted to digging deep and working hard to open up and try something different.

My new nurse counsellor, Joan, had the reputation of being strict and brisk. At first glance, she had the demeanour of an old schoolmarm, and I later found out that she'd been a charge nurse in a busy hospital for a short time. This was in the days when charge nurses ran their unit and everyone on it, including the doctors. They were not to be trifled with and this woman fit the bill. When Joan called me a piece of work, it was a gift. She wasn't going to take any crap from me. She knew the ropes. She'd been there. She could spot my tendencies to blame, hide, get angry, or deflect with humour, and she seemed unafraid of me or how I might respond when she called me out. I respected her and her willingness to confront me head-on. I wanted a battle-hardened fighter who would shoot back. I wanted a person who'd done what I was trying to do and knew firsthand what they were asking of me—to let go of my toughness and allow a more vulnerable side to emerge. Joan was tough and I was tough. I could trust her.

And yet, as I discovered, Joan could also be very gentle. She'd tell me I was sensitive and I would furrow my brow. I didn't believe I was sensitive—I'd been working hard to present as anything but! Joan saw past my hard shell and seemed to sense that underneath was a sad woman avoiding pain. She knew how to meet me where I was on any given day and invite me to feel more, to be gentle with myself, and to sit with discomfort rather than get busy "figuring things out."

I discovered with Joan and Brenda that I'd gotten comfortable with taking a "cognitive approach" to just about everything in order to avoid sitting with my feelings. I spent more time in my head than in my heart.

As I got to know Joan better, I learned that her no-nonsense exterior wasn't representative of her whole personality. She was also a tenderhearted, thoughtful, and spiritual woman who took her calling to work with broken mothers very seriously. She was committed to sharing her experience and expertise in an unreserved manner; in the spirit of service, she was willing to stand up to angry mothers. She helped countless mothers who, like me, needed someone to show them a way out of feeling defeated and hopeless. Again, thank goodness for women like Joan.

If you're seeking help and finding that your practitioner is not a good fit for where you are emotionally, be clear and honest about it. You can do this with compassion. You may feel intimidated or even feel like you need to protect your practitioner's feelings by pretending all is well but you *must* be honest if you're to make good use of your time with them. Open up to them about what is happening, your doubts about the treatment approach, and what you're looking for. It may be a case in which there is a misunderstanding. Try to stay open as you advocate for yourself.

Reflective Questions:
- Do you have an attitude that is getting in the way of seeking and accepting help?
- If so, where is it coming from? Is there something else in the way of you truly hearing those who are trying to help you?
- Can you ask for, or meditate on, becoming more willing to accept help and do what you need to do to change?

CHAPTER SIXTEEN

Over the years, I've reflected on the adversity I've experienced in my life. I've worn successes as a badge of honour in light of the adversity I'd experienced in my childhood home. I'm proud I grew up to have a family, that I married a great man, and that I became a nurse. Overcoming my circumstances felt like a very personal victory. There was a time when I didn't talk about my childhood but when I started to, people seemed surprised that I'd come from an adverse background. There was a part of me that relished their amazement, and I began to feel righteous and special to have succeeded where others may have failed.

As we raised the kids and I returned to school twice, I soaked up the validation that others gave me. It made me feel superhuman. People would say, "Wow, I don't know how you do it," and that would feed my ego and cement my identity as an especially strong person capable of handling more adversity than the average bear. While this wasn't my motivation for going back to school, I did enjoy the idea that I was somehow super capable. Steve and I both worked hard, managed a busy home, and raised the kids; on top of that, he completed several marathons and I achieved two degrees. I came to love my laundry list of hardships, especially when I held it up against our achievements.

As my comfort with group therapy increased, I wanted more and more time to share, especially when Natalie was working. Natalie is a petite, sharp, kind, and assertive fireball who shared the role of clinical director at AARC. I loved the way she challenged us, both kids and parents, and I felt like I made great strides in understanding addiction and recovery when she was working. My trust for her was huge and because of that, I could be very, very honest and really dig into things that bothered me, even sharing in front of the entire parent group. She seemed never to be fazed, always infinitely patient, and at the same time very honest and straightforward with her insights.

One evening in January 2014, Steve and I were once again in parent group, and as I stood against the wall looking out at the faces of the parents sitting in chairs, I could feel myself getting antsy. We'd been asked to reflect on a time when we'd become exhausted and felt like giving up. That was an easy one. I looked forward to sharing. I put my hand up and was invited to talk. I started with the stories of having Ben live with us and move out each time he used. I described the wearing down of our resolve, the getting to the end of our rope each time it happened, and how we always eventually changed our minds and invited him to live with us again despite our vow not to. This was a good example of feeling exhausted, I thought, because it let me add in all the things happening with Sam and Ally at the same time. I was really getting into it, really relishing the little shakes of other parents' heads as they took in the exceptional level of chaos we'd endured.

As often happened in these sessions, the theme of the evening started to change as people shared their stories. Natalie began asking questions, digging into the level of frustration I was describing, and as other parents contributed their own stories, she encouraged us to talk about our feelings when we experienced the futility of one failed intervention after another. I reflected on my anger and frustration and what was really behind it.

Part of it was the feeling of being cheated. I'd put my time in with my boys. I'd held up my end of the unspoken bargain to raise them to adulthood. But they'd failed to uphold their end to successfully transition into independent adults who were functional either in work or in getting an education. They'd cheated me out of feeling like a successful mother. They'd sucked up time and energy I would've given to my career and life's purpose. I remember saying that night, "I am here on Earth to do more than just be a mom of addicts, and I feel robbed of all my time and energy. I have nothing left." Then I pulled out my old laundry list of hardships, starting with my family of origin, as evidence that I'd indeed faced more than average adversity and was very justified in my frustration and anger. I'd been battling adversity all my life and it just wasn't fair!

Then Natalie told us a story. She talked about being one of five children and described visiting home for a family supper when she was a young adult. She was in recovery from addictions and doing well, but she said one of her siblings was still using and missing in action. As she and her three healthy siblings sat and tried to visit as a family, their mother spent her time and energy lamenting the absence of the other child, who was still sick and using drugs and alcohol. She described it as "such as shame" that her mother couldn't enjoy the presence of her four healthy kids, instead focusing on the child who wasn't there.

I immediately felt my heart start to race and my temperature rise. I became flushed with anger and indignation. "I'm feeling a little defensive of your mother," I told her. She nodded and let me continue. "You spent years wearing her down and you have the nerve to be critical of her sadness? Of course, she had trouble celebrating. She'd spent years trying to save you all, to no avail."

Natalie nodded again. She agreed that all of that was true—her mother was tired and had every right to hang on to her sadness and focus on the absent child. She agreed that it was a terrible shame they couldn't be together that evening because her sibling was still struggling. But, she added, listening to her mother was an eye-opener. She noted that her mother had a choice to either focus on the four healthy children in front of her and enjoy them in that moment or to focus on the one child who wasn't there and let that interfere with her relationship with the healthy kids. "You have every right to be tired, frustrated, and feel a victim of your adversity," Natalie said then. "You are more than entitled to dwell on it as long as you like. But I have to ask you, is that what you want for yourself?"

She stopped me dead in my tracks. She was pointing out that while I had been through a lot, I had a choice in how I proceeded from there or even if I was willing to proceed at all. I was a little uncomfortable, at first, with this idea of choice. I felt challenged to consider another way to live, one that I hadn't seen before. I felt challenged to consider letting go of my laundry list, to live a life that focused on what I could control: my attitude and willingness to celebrate what was going well.

I immediately thought of my daughters and particularly of Sydney, then 17, who hadn't needed anything extraordinary from us. In fact, she'd done her best not to need even ordinary parenting. Sydney's an introvert. And she's one of the smartest, wittiest, most independent people I know. She has a busy mind and a soft heart, which she protects by projecting a quiet and calm demeanor. She's a keen observer, an efficient and hard worker, and she has a busy intellectual mind. She is an avid reader, offering insightful critiques of literature when asked. She lights up when she talks about books, ideas, and when she witnesses something like the honesty of preschoolers when we're out in public. She says she finds the unreserved display of their emotions endearing and amusing.

Sydney likes to stay in control of her feelings. Occasionally, I see them pop to the surface, though she's quick to rein them back in again. She's a talented sketch artist who keeps much of her work private. And she's a sharp advocate for kids and anyone she sees as an underdog.

When she was a teenager, I rationalized that her time in her room was just "recharging," but I know now it was more like hiding from the chaos and that she, too, was suffering. I felt guilty for not having considered this before. I thought about a typical evening in our home when Sydney would quietly disappear to her room. I'd knock or pop my head in to say goodnight, silently grateful. I felt like I didn't have to worry about her like I did the other kids. My heart sank considering how this might have been for her, watching her siblings take up all our time and energy, and us just letting them have it, one crisis at a time, over the course of years, until there was nothing left for her. I just wasn't focused on Syd, who I thought had been doing well in school and water polo and who was becoming a gifted artist. I'd missed her formative teen years completely. I resolved then to spend more time with her as soon as the program at AARC was finished.

I reflected that evening at AARC on how little time or energy I'd spent dwelling on success or what there was to be grateful for. In fact, gratitude seemed a very abstract concept to me; it was so far from my consciousness. I was quiet for the rest of that evening as the weight of Natalie's story sunk in. The internal debate began as I vacillated between justifying my anger at the "hand I'd been dealt" and repeating Natalie's question. Was that fixation on my victimhood really what I wanted for myself? I began to see that it was keeping me stuck in resentment and the list of hardships would just keep getting longer as life went on. In fact, everyone could have a list and we could keep adding to it. We all face adversity. Over the coming days and weeks, I slowly began to believe that I really did have a choice. But letting go of my comfortable identity as a victim of—and victor over—adversity was difficult. The mentality had become pretty ingrained. I'd been making my lists and constructing my story about being tougher-than-average for a long time.

I made the decision to try to spend some time focusing on what was going well. I decided to find things to be grateful for and take a moment each day to acknowledge them. Some days, this was really tough. I felt negative one morning and I was in a hurry to get through rush-hour traffic. I was stuck on a major roadway in Calgary, in barely crawling traffic, feeling my anxiety mount as I realized I was going to be late. My internal narrative began with, "Here we go, just one more thing. This mess is ruining my morning." But in a moment of grace, I noticed that I was only adding to the negative event with my cruddy perspective. I decided in that moment to try something different.

This was an opportunity to focus on what was going well instead of circumstances that were beyond my control. But the dark cloud of my outlook had been following me up the highway and all my life and my negativity was hard to ignore. As I sat there looking at the frustrated drivers all around me, I tried to find something to be grateful for. I searched my mind for something to feel happy about. I struggled, looking from the drivers to the blue sky, and I thought, "That's it, I guess. I can be grateful for the blue sky." It was a start, a moment in which I realized if I could only come up with the sky as something that I was grateful for, I had a lot of work to do. Even then, I knew the big blue sky couldn't be the only good thing in my life. I vowed to keep practicing gratitude in an effort to shift my focus and become increasingly aware of my many blessings.

This new willingness to focus on gratitude, on what's going well, and to spend my energy on thinking about and appreciating things, slowly began to change me. I felt more empowered as I thought about things that I appreciated, and I made the decision, over and over again, to feel grateful for those things. The tough feelings didn't go away but the anger, frustration, and feeling of being trapped in a life I didn't choose began to subside.

Pain is pain, and sadness is sadness, and today, I know that when I accept those feelings, love them for their contrast to joy, and then refocus my energy on noticing positive things and doing things that make me healthy, I feel better. I feel joy. Gratitude comes more easily. Today, when I feel pain and sadness, I take the time to rest, share with friends, or walk the dog. I plan something fun or spend time with any one of my kids (ideally, all of them). I can offer a stranger a compliment or buy someone a coffee and this generosity changes me.

I hear victim stories all the time—in talking with friends, facilitating leadership programs, or running my own program with parents. It's a natural human tendency, I think, to complain about things that aren't happening the way we like. I fall into it too. But when I remember Natalie—"Is this what you want for yourself?"—I stop. Complaining is the hallmark of victimhood and recognizing our choice to change the story we tell about ourselves is the gateway to freedom.

Reflections:
- Where and when do you feel like a victim of other people, events, or circumstance?
- Often, we use our victim stories as a rationale for our unpleasant feelings. Does this have a ring of truth for you? Journal for five minutes about what is true for you.
- Offer yourself acceptance and validation in your journal for the feelings you are having.
- Where is there room for choice in your story? (Hint: there is more room than you think).
- What is the feeling you would like to create more of in your life?
- What do you need to consider, think about, and focus on more often to get more of your desired feelings?
- What small actions can you commit to?

CHAPTER SEVENTEEN

Homecoming is an important milestone in the AARC recovery program. Your children are permitted to come home in the evenings and take on more of a leadership role to newer kids in treatment. It's a huge celebration and the exact date is a surprise to parents and siblings. After months of having our children go to other people's homes, we were acknowledged as a family far enough along in the program to host other kids and practice having our own kids home while trying to stay out of their recovery and simply act as parents.

Steve was out of town working on the cold February evening that Ben surprised us with his homecoming. After an emotional celebration at AARC, we were sent home to spend some time together as a family. We were given a few days off from hosting other kids so we could just focus on our own children, and to make the most of it, I made plans to take the kids to laser tag. Ally declined, saying she just didn't feel up to it, which wasn't unusual for her. She was choosy about activities. We were disappointed but Sam, Ben, Sydney, and I went off to have a fun evening trying to shoot each other in a dark maze. When we arrived home, we faced another crisis.

We found Ally sitting alone in the front room. The lights were off and she was just a shadow on the sofa. I asked how she was feeling. She said she "wasn't feeling well," had called the kids' help line, and the police were on their way. She'd confided to the help line that she had thoughts of self-harm so the protocol was to have her assessed for suicidality. I sighed, trying to control my frustration. This changed everything, once again, in an instant. The celebration was over, as was our homecoming weekend.

The police arrived a few minutes later, flashing lights and all, and interviewed Ally and I separately. Sam, Ben, and Sydney sat in the kitchen quietly, and the police decided that Ally needed to be assessed at the hospital to be sure she was safe from hurting herself. I needed to follow, and I quickly phoned the on-call counsellors at AARC so that Sam and Ben could be picked up and taken to another home for the night. As I was on the phone and the police were standing in our front foyer with Ally, Sam sidled up to me and asked in a low voice, "Can I talk to you for a second?" This was a question I'd heard from him with increasing frequency as he struggled with his own feelings over the past year or two. I took a deep breath and quietly turned to him and said, "No. I'm in the middle of dealing with something, Sam." He stepped away.

Now that I have a better understanding of BPD, I have some idea about why both Sam and Ally struggled that night and why they both presented as needing time and attention during an otherwise fun family evening meant to celebrate their sibling. Emotions run to the extreme in those with BPD, both up and down. And it's overwhelming. Ben's homecoming prompted a lot of feelings in all of us. It was an exciting and scary few days. Traditionally, Sam would've used drugs to cope and Ally would've cut. But Sam was sober and in treatment and Ally was trying not to self-harm but the urge was strong, prompting her call to the helpline.

At the time, both of them seemed to be making every effort to make their brother's celebration about themselves—it seemed manipulative and selfish—two words often associated with BPD. I think this is a huge misunderstanding. Behaviours that are often interpreted as manipulative and selfish are actually an indication that a person is overwhelmed and is trying to process their feelings in an unproductive way.

After Ben and Sam were picked up, I left in the car to follow the police and Ally to the hospital. Once again, Syd was left alone to cope on her own. I felt tired, frustrated, and embarrassed. We were on an endless cycle of one step forward and two steps back. I was sick of it. I called Heather, a friend from AARC, on my drive and talked with her about what a disruptive "waste of time" I thought this trip was. I told her I didn't think Ally needed to be hospitalized. In fact, I thought that hospitalization was the last thing she needed. Ally was overwhelmed and needed help processing her feelings. I thought she needed to use the mindfulness skills she'd learned in DBT. She didn't need a drastic intervention to keep her safe. In my mind, she was as safe as ever. I felt like I knew her and her moods fairly well by this time, and I was sure that if I'd just been home for the evening, or home a little bit sooner, all this could've been avoided.

Heather was another no-nonsense woman. She was fun, loud, brash, and underneath it all, I discovered, very soft and loving. She had a way of saying my name that I found endearing—she used two distinct syllables, "Mo-reen."

She suggested to me that I let others decide on the best course of action. "Just let the pros take care of it. They'll decide if Ally needs to be hospitalized or sent home." For years, I'd been trying to impose my will regarding the best course of action with emergency and temporary care providers. We'd crossed paths with many of them, from police, paramedics, and emergency department staff to on-call doctors, resident doctors, and short-term and temporary counsellors. There'd been so many people involved that I had trouble trusting they'd be able to sort through our long and complicated history. I wasn't convinced that, in their brief encounter with us, they'd make sound decisions that were in line with those of our "regular" psychiatrists, psychologists, and treatment centres. I'd felt the need to fill them all in, and a few times, to fight to keep us all on track.

I decided to take Heather's advice and trust others to figure it out and go from there. What a relief! She gave me permission to relax and just be a mom, to stop being a case manager. I could let the staff at the children's hospital do their job. I could offer my opinion and let go of the pressure of getting them to make the "right" decision. I could trust that whatever *they* decided was the right decision.

I sat in a small room at the emergency department of the children's hospital with Ally. The lights were bright, unforgiving, and I was aware that I was wearing the emotional toll of the past few days on my face. When I saw my reflection in the bathroom mirror, I looked as tired as I felt. In walked a stranger with a clipboard to gather a history. I took a deep breath and steeled myself. This was a discouraging process at the best of times, and tonight, I was feeling rather defeated.

I let Ally answer her questions first, and when it came time for family history, I made my best effort to make the chaos of the past few years sound clear and uncomplicated. It didn't work. I could see the confusion and disbelief on the professional-of-the-day's face. Her expression seemed to border on judgement, and I immediately steeled myself, redoubling my efforts to sound rational. I feared once again that rather than be supported by the system, I'd be judged by it. I hearkened back to Ally's diagnosis in her psychiatrist's office and how overlooked I felt in my struggle as a caregiver who was overwhelmed and feeling a little crazy myself. I needed help but didn't feel like I could or should ask for it.

We made it through the few hours of assessment without incident and, to my relief, we were sent home. I was a little angry that we'd been cheated out of a nice family evening, especially now that Ally seemed in reasonably good spirits. I thought about my counsellor, Joan, and looked forward to talking with her about the night and having her help me process my feelings. She always helped me to accept myself, accept others, and let go. But for now, it was clear that Ally and I were both tired. The drive home was quiet, both of us a little reflective. It was after midnight and I felt relieved when I crawled into bed.

Takeaway Points:
- When there are mental health and addictions in a family, the family members and the family system are deeply affected.
- Caregivers, in particular, bear the burden of case-managing and supporting the sick individual, sometimes to the detriment of their own mental and physical health.
- When caregivers experience distress and present to physicians or other service providers with physical and emotional complaints, they're met with varying levels of understanding, empathy, and ability to find or refer to the resources needed. The caregiver may feel overlooked or judged by health care providers.
- Resources that provide solutions for a dysfunctional family dynamic are often in short supply.
- Caregivers in particular experience a higher-than-usual rate of distress and mental health issues. Even when symptoms may not be severe enough to be diagnosed, they interfere with the health and

functioning of that caregiver and, possibly, the caregiver's entire family: an ailing caregiver becomes increasingly unavailable to other family members.

- The stress over time of chronic mental illness and addictions may challenge a family system to the point where collective strength and support is lost as multiple family members struggle with their own mental health issues.

- Further, there can be a cyclical effect of caregiver distress on the "patient." Distress for caregivers and their families increases with the following factors: secrecy, isolation, a decrease in support systems, time off work, increased work hours, and increased out-of-pocket expenses.

- Sometimes family members will not present with "mental health problems" per se because they can't afford to be ill or not coping.

- Stigma and a lack of understanding can lead to families concealing problems and perhaps distancing themselves from each other, their friends, and the wider community. Therefore, the needs of families can remain unidentified, ultimately to the detriment of the caregiver and the family system.

- Family members' and caregivers' mental health needs to become a priority in our system, and caregivers need to be understood as more than just people who provide context to the "patient's story."[7]

Endnotes

7   Family Mental Health Alliance (FMHA). (2006). "Caring together: families as partners in the mental health and addiction system."

Kuhn, Emily S, and Laird, Robert D. July 10, 2014. "Family support programs and adolescent mental health: review of evidence.:

Robinson, E., Rodgers, B., and Butterworth, P. (2008). "Family relationships and mental illness: impacts and service responses." Australian Family Relationships Clearinghouse.

Statistics Canada. (2015). "Health at a glance: the impact of mental health problems on family members."

CHAPTER EIGHTEEN

After that evening in the emergency department and over the next few months, Ally didn't seem to be making significant progress. She'd stopped seeing her counsellor at Inner Solutions, at her choice, and we seemed to be in a bit of a holding pattern. The boys appeared to be improving with AARC's 12-Step model, but Ally was up and down, and when she did cut, some of it was deep enough that I worried she'd accidentally hit an artery and bleed to death before she could ask for help. I worried about how quickly this could happen and I felt frantic thinking about her alone and dying.

I'd tried various techniques to control her self-harm, like asking her for all sharp objects before leaving her alone in her room, checking her room myself, and randomly checking her arms, all to no avail. There seemed to be no noticeable improvement with my increasing interventions and attempts to keep her safe. One day, I had the idea of turning her bedroom into a "recovery room" modeled after the AARC's Recovery Home. This included a mattress on the floor, an alarmed window, and an alarmed door. I bought an alarm and, before installing it, had a chat with Natalie, the counselor at AARC. I wanted to advocate for a 12-Step program for BPD. The recovery program I'd seen as a part of AARC seemed like a great option for Ally. She wasn't an addict, though, so I needed to convince AARC to start a specialized program for her. I knew of other kids and siblings in the program that self-harmed so I was confident that if AARC started a program, they'd have no shortage of clients.

As I sat down on the comfortable sofa in Natalie's spacious office, I started in on my spiel about what I thought AARC needed to do for Ally and our family. Natalie listened but when I finished, she simply said, "That's not going to happen." I wasn't all that surprised, and I told her about my backup plan to create a recovery room for Ally as a solution. Natalie again listened, then responded with, "That's not normal, Maureen. It's an extreme intervention and no way to live."

"Well, what am I to do, then?"

She replied calmly and with remarkable compassion. She looked me in the eyes and said, "You need to accept that you cannot control what Ally does. You need to accept that she may even die if she continues to cut."

I remember thinking, "No, I don't." But I sat there and let it sink in a little before heading home.

After relaying the conversation to Steve, we decided that Natalie was right. We didn't want to take our attempts to control and manage Ally to extremes like turning her room into a "safe room." It wasn't likely to work anyway. If she wanted to cut, she'd find a way, interventions or not.

Over the coming weeks and months, Natalie's encouragement to work on acceptance slowly sunk in. I'd learned a fair amount about acceptance when it came to the boys but I was now challenged to apply those same principles to Ally. This was the beginning of a real turning point in my approach to Ally's mental illness. I started to accept my own fear and my own lack of control. I started to accept her struggles in a new way and appreciate her efforts to get better.

My acceptance of my kids' paths would be challenged repeatedly.

In May, after earning a level of freedom and independence in the AARC program, Sam was in the middle of his daily chores when he walked out to the parking lot and just kept going. Steve had an appointment at AARC that same day and when he arrived, he was told that Sam was missing. Sam had had at least one suicide attempt while in the program, on top of the attempts before treatment. He was a high risk for suicide. Steve called me at work and said the police had been notified and were reportedly on the way to our home to search the house. The girls were home alone after school, and I felt a little panicky, thinking of them facing the police on their own and getting the news from them that Sam was missing.

Strangely, I also thought about how messy our house was and felt a flush of embarrassment that strangers would be walking through it. I immediately headed for home, calling the girls on the way. I wanted to be there before the police arrived. This felt like way too much to ask them to handle and my heart ached for them, even as it sank while I considered Sam's potential state of mind.

The police car was parked at the curb. The girls had let the police inside and they'd searched the house—no Sam.

The police then proceeded to search the nearby Bow River, thinking that maybe Sam had jumped in. The Bow is turbulent and dangerous in areas. Many lives have ended in that river and without much else to go on, that seemed like the next best place to look. I heard the police helicopter in the sky and couldn't believe how serious this was. It was a horrible, long afternoon spent hoping Sam would turn up safe. Ben was supported in treatment and Steve had AARC support as well. I made a call to Brenda for support and talked about how I felt, the fear and sadness washing over me. I hung up the phone and asked the girls to have a snuggle in an oversized chair. They obliged, and we talked about how scary it was that Sam might not be okay. I cried as we talked and then one of the girls said, "Mom, you've changed."

I agreed. I had changed. I asked them what they saw that was different.

"I don't know...you're less terrifying now," she said.

That hit hard! Terrifying? That's how I'd seemed to them in the past when I thought I was being strong? I thought I'd been protecting them by not showing or talking about my fears and sadness over the years. I thought I'd been stoic, strong, and steady in the face of other people's scary and unpredictable behaviours. The girls were now telling me that I'd been *contributing* to the scary and unpredictable behaviours. This was undeniable confirmation to me that my behaviours had indeed done some damage, and not only did I need to open up my feelings of fear and sadness to myself, I had to open them up to the kids too. It was hard to hear "terrifying" used to describe me.

The day that Sam went missing, I was calm, accepting, and sad, even as I cried with the girls. And they seemed to open up too. I felt closer to them then and I pledged to be more demonstrative with my feelings. It felt safe and honest. I could let my feelings show and talk about them. I realized then that I could be an example to them that it was okay to feel, talk openly, and be, in a word, human. It was crystal clear that day that it was much scarier for the kids when I acted like I didn't have feelings. I'd been wrong in thinking my kids would find my fear and sadness most unsettling.

Sam called me a few hours later, at about 5:00 p.m., on the prompting of a good friend of his. It turns out, he'd met that friend for coffee. What a relief—he was okay. He said he didn't want to go back to AARC and was reluctant to tell me where he was because he thought I might come and "force" him to return. I promised this wasn't the case. He told me he was at a Tim Horton's, and I called the police to let them know. The search was called off.

I stopped by the coffee shop to see Sam on my way to AARC, where we were still supporting Ben in treatment, and gave him a hug. He seemed guarded to me—he was still nervous that I would make him go back to treatment. I again promised that I wouldn't, and when I told him that I wished him well if he chose to leave treatment and that I needed to go to AARC for a meeting that night, his eyes widened and he shifted in his seat. He had not been expecting acceptance from me.

It was difficult to leave him there, and I cried again as I drove to AARC for the evening Parent Rap. I had learned at AARC to accept my lack of control, to let things unfold as they would and trust that they would work out as they were meant to, and to focus on my own feelings. Sam's future was uncertain, and I was worried for him.

Later that night, he reached out to another AARC family who had finished treatment and asked if he could stay with them. The mother, who'd become a friend of mine, texted me to let me know. To my eternal gratitude, they told him the best option was to return to treatment and that was the only option they would support. He agreed and they drove him back to the centre. He signed himself back into treatment near midnight.

I had always tried to jump in, get involved, and act. I'd analyse the issue, figure out the options, and fight hard for one I wanted. By summer, I'd begun to trust that there was a better way to respond to things that upset or scared me. I'd dabbled in letting go but I still struggled with inaction. It left me still enough to feel my emotions. I had also associated inaction as passivity and resignation and that, in my mind, was too close to being "weak."

But I was learning from other parents and staff in the program that acceptance was synonymous with freedom, not weakness.

I began to realize I had other traits counterproductive to growth and freedom. Arrogance, rationalization, and self-pity were top of the list. I wanted to let them go. However, to my surprise, I felt attached to them. As it turned out, I kind of *liked* rationalizing my behaviours. I kind of *liked* my self-pity. I *liked* feeling arrogant and superior. It was ugly to admit but it was true. Letting go of attachment and my learned behaviours was harder than I expected.

I've been a student of behavioural change, emotional intelligence, and leadership since 2009, and I believe that our learned behaviours serve to protect us. We learn how to behave beginning at a very young age. Our behaviors become set and more ingrained as they're repeated. Children are highly adaptive and learn ways to avoid pain and get their needs met. Behaviour is a consequence of nature (the genetics a child is born with) and nurture (the environment a child lives in and the reinforcement a child receives). Every child needs attention and approval and will behave in ways that get both positive and negative attention and approval. We learn our competitive, conflict avoidant, aggressive, or passive traits very young. We come by our behaviours honestly because they're necessary and they work well for us, until they don't.[8]

Most of us have felt the frustration of not knowing how to change a pattern we've developed. We regret the way we handle something and yet we do it again. When it came to the idea of letting go of my attempts to control the things and people around me, I was afraid it might make me weak. This fear of weakness could be traced back to my family of origin. It was so ingrained into who I was that I didn't see a way to both be me *and* let go of my old behaviours. I had Brenda, Joan, and the entire recovery community at AARC telling me I'd be okay, even happier and more joyful, but it took some real faith to let go and try.

That July, I attended a breakfast event I helped organize for AARC. The Calgary Stampede is an annual 10-day event with a Western rodeo theme. Most businesses use the opportunity to host a free breakfast event to garner promotion and encourage networking and good public relations. During the organizing phase, I had experienced some conflict working with the AARC staff member assigned to oversee the parent committee.

I'd been very judgemental of the staff member and I'd provoked her in the planning meetings by challenging her authority in front of the other parents. I deliberately pushed her to raise her voice.

Now that the event was underway, I was half-heartedly trying to get along with her, even despite our low-lying contention. But then she admonished me for something that wasn't my fault. I felt wronged and I struggled to keep my cool. I walked through the hallways of the centre considering how to let go and behave in a new way. I was rationalizing and feeling very righteous, very angry. I rounded a corner quickly, only to find my first nurse counsellor, the one I'd decided was too soft to help me, relaxing alone in a chair. She'd left the center by then and was attending the event as a guest.

I said hello. When she asked how I was doing, I said I was struggling with something. True to her nature, she generously gave me her time and her ear. She leaned forward in her jeans and cowboy hat and invited me to share. The hallway was quiet. It was just her and me. By then, I'd begun to change, to soften, and I was finally open to the help that she'd always been offering but that I'd been resistant to. She listened. Repeatedly, she asked, "What's your part, Maureen?" until I admitted that I had provoked this woman. I'd been righteous and indignant, and immature.

"So what do you need to do now?" she asked.

"I need to apologize," I answered. She helped me muster the courage to apologize for my role in the conflict. It took courage to be vulnerable with someone that I didn't like very much and in a situation in which I felt like I had been wronged as well.

Where I rationalized my behaviours that contributed to the conflict, the counsellor challenged me to admit I'd been wrong. She asked me to take responsibility for my actions. She helped me to let go of the expectation of an apology. Depending on another person to apologize and accept accountability meant putting my freedom in another person's hands. She conveyed all this by simply and repeatedly asking the question, "What was your part?" It was brilliant. She forced me to focus on myself and where I'd been wrong. She was gentle and she was firm, and I began to see her in a different light that day, one that wasn't clouded by my previously closed mind.

This was my chance to try something different. It was intense and very difficult to apologize while my emotions still ran high. As I approached the woman with whom I'd had conflict, I took a big breath and with humility and honesty, I apologized for being confrontational weeks before. I apologized for provoking her and making the planning of the event difficult. As I spoke, I struggled to hold back my tears. It was hard to be humble with this woman. But her face visibly softened and she hugged me. She also appeared to be holding back tears. Clearly, the conflict had taken a toll on her as well, and I felt bad for that but also happy I'd done what I could to clean it up.

As I walked away, I felt strong. I didn't feel weak or passive. I felt accountable and courageous.

On that day, I learned, among other things, that when I take responsibility for myself, when I focus on behaving in ways that are in line with who I want to be and let go of trying to manage and change others, I truly step into the possibility of my own freedom.

The easiest way to maintain my freedom today is to focus on my own values. For example, if my values include honesty, courage, and accountability, I reflect on what behaviours reflect those values. I still have frustrations and conflict, but as long as I behave in a way that reflects who I am and what is important to me, I am on track and I can keep my own "side of the street" clean.

Reflective Questions:
- Changing old patterns can be difficult, even when we know they're holding us back from growing. There is fear of the unknown and a comfort in the devil you know! Reflect on what you stand to lose by letting go of your old patterns that no longer serve you.
- Journal on the thought that taking accountability for your role in dysfunction somehow might make others who are not innocent believe that they've "won."
- Where is there a falseness in your thinking?
- What is true?

Endnotes

8   https://www.verywellmind.com/what-is-child-psychology-2795067

https://www.psychologytoday.com/intl/blog/when-your-adult-child-breaks-your-heart/201712/understanding-your-childs-behaviors-in-context

https://www.psychologytoday.com/intl/blog/stress-free-discipline/201509/the-abcs-child-behavior

CHAPTER NINETEEN

Over a 12-month period in 2014, starting while our family was still in AARC, I participated in a research study on the experience of mothering addicted kids. Jackie, a PhD candidate at the University of Calgary who was also a nurse counsellor at AARC, was the researcher and author and we talked about my experience. We discussed my own mom at length, how she wasn't the strong, protective, and independent mom I wanted. I was angry at her because of that and I vowed to be different.

In my mind, my mother's greatest failure was her inability to protect us from our father. I used to fantasize that she'd pack us up and we'd leave home. We'd finally be free of his tyrannical behaviour and abuse. But she didn't do that. As far as I could see, she didn't do anything to mitigate the damage he did; in fact, she was devoted to him. She reinforced many of his messages, literally parroting his words. She had an unwillingness to really look at the ugly truths of our home. She was willfully ignorant about the damage being done by my father, turning a blind eye. To me, this made her complicit in his abuse of us.

Further, her devotion to him had me scratching my head (if not shaking it in disgust). I didn't understand her. I was determined to be strong as a mom and stand up for my own kids—to anyone and everyone.

As I described my childhood home, Jackie asked me what I thought what it might've been like for my mother. I drew a blank. I had no idea.

My mother was, and is, an enigma to me. I found her to be emotionally flat and difficult to read. As a kid, I only remember her repeating my dad's opinions. As an adult, I asked about her childhood in the hopes of getting to know her better. I probed for details and got vague answers and flippancy. I could only suppose that our family home was difficult for her. She was also a victim of my dad's violence. And then, quite suddenly, it hit me.

My mother had married and had children, and I think that even though she made best efforts to create a happy home, life went sideways. I remember her reading to us and making meals for us. And still, things happened that were beyond her control. I'd married and had children, too, and despite my best efforts to create a happy, healthy home, life went sideways. Things happened that were beyond my control.

Hmmmm. While our behaviours within these scenarios differed greatly, the fact remained: My mother and I had something in common. I considered that we both did our best given the tools we had and we still couldn't control what happened. And she, like me, may even look back and wish she'd done things differently. My mother and I are very different but this was my first glimpse that we had *anything* in common and it was enough to put a crack in my shell. This realization hit me hard. I cried as I talked to Jackie about it.

As I reflect, I wonder if my mom felt the same about her own mother, who was more like me. My grandmother was strong, assertive, *and* emotionally unavailable. I related to her and I still feel very close to her many years after her death in 1995. But I wonder if my mom struggled with her mom and was determined to be "nothing like her" too. What if everyone, from every generation, observes their parents and decides to be different, sometimes swinging the pendulum too far in the opposite direction?

Regardless, I consider today how righteous I'd been to think that I could be better than anyone else as a parent. That my "superior" mothering that would result in a superior outcome. Boy, had I blown that little experiment. This was a critical first step in forgiving my mother. I began to consider that although it wasn't okay for her to let me be abused, she'd done her best. We both ended up in situations we certainly didn't plan for.

Participating in that research was pivotal for me in understanding who I was as a mom. I was fascinated with the process and enjoyed talking with Jackie and the other participants. I learned that we all had different experiences and interpretations of mothering. I was hungry to unearth who I really was as a mom of addicted kids.

I was challenged when Jackie asked me to bring in objects I thought represented me as a mom. Again, it was easier to define myself by what I opposed than by what I valued and loved about motherhood. As Jackie's research came to a close, she wrote me a note, using my own words from our conversations, that articulated, finally, how I saw myself as a mom. Tears came to my eyes as I read it. It was the closest I'd ever come to knowing who I was in relation to my kids. It read:

> I am a mother who loves her kids. I am not my kids' solution and it is not my responsibility to save them, but I am a mother who loves them.
>
> I am a mother who loves enough to let go and who is learning to stand back and allow other people to help my kids help themselves. I have learned that the solution is to look after myself and let others do the same.
>
> I am a mother like other mothers who struggles to relate to her kids. I may not relate to the pearls and aprons, but I do relate to the story of a mother who wants to support and save her kids. That is what we have in common.
>
> I am a mother who is facing the fears, anger, and sadness of her past and who is learning to use awareness and acceptance rather than anger and reactiveness.
>
> I am not a victim, but rather a loving mother of sons with substance addictions, who feels able to support her children in a recovery process that she understands better today. I am safe now to let go of the imaginary reins that I have been using to try and steer my children's lives.

Reflective Questions:

- What aspect of your childhood do you want to recreate?
- What aspect of your childhood home are/were you determined not to recreate?
- Do you believe that everyone is doing their best, including you? If so, how can you nurture compassion for any shortcomings?
- How do you define yourself as a parent, child, sibling, friend?

CHAPTER TWENTY

When Sydney graduated from high school in June 2014, I thought back to all the times she'd gone quietly to her room while we focused on the other three kids. This was an opportunity to just focus on her, and Steve and I offered her a choice for a graduation gift. She could choose a new laptop (our traditional graduation gift) or a trip with me to Canada's Wonderland, an amusement park in Ontario. I remember her face lighting up as she immediately said she preferred the trip. It warmed my heart to see her excitement. I felt excited to have time with her. I am grateful to this day that she chose the trip and so grateful to Steve for supporting us both in going.

Sydney and I flew to Toronto, rented a car, and headed for the park. We stayed in a nice hotel. We relished our time in restaurants. We enjoyed the luxury of our comfy beds. On the plane, Sydney had watched an episode of a show called *You Should Eat Here* about a new restaurant in downtown Toronto. The restaurant was tiny and tucked away in the financial district. The streets were quiet on the long weekend, and when we found the restaurant, we were excited to find it open for business. We stepped into the small entryway and told the hostess that we sought them out because we'd seen them on the show. She smiled, disappeared, and came back with the owner who came out to say hello, seat us at the bar, and send us a complimentary dish, their signature macaroni and cheese. We felt like celebrities.

We bought a Toronto Blue Jays blanket, parked our car, and hiked along with many other Torontonians to the beach of Lake Ontario to watch the Canada Day fireworks. And we spent two full days at Wonderland. It wasn't crowded and we were able to ride our favourite rollercoasters repeatedly. The whole trip was amazing. We even tried a ride that had us freefalling and then shooting out over the park in a little sling. I have a picture of us on this ride, and it's one of my favourite memories.

It was a short trip, a drop in the bucket relative to all the time I owed her, but I relished the experience. I smile when I remember what a small but special thing it was to go there with her, just the two of us. No drama and no distractions, just a ton of fun. One of my favourite pictures is of Sydney's face as she watched a life-size Snoopy get up to conduct a symphony in the middle of the park. Her expression was pure joy and such innocence. She was 17 years old and still had the wide-eyed wonder of a four-year-old.

When we talk about that trip today, we both recount the details with smiles. It was a bright light for us, coming out of years of darkness in our home. We carried with us none of the heaviness that we'd been living with for so long. I would love to do it again with her.

The theories on the varying roles that members of a family take on when there is addiction in a home were first identified by Sharon Weischeider in 1981. The roles include the caretaker or enabler, the scapegoat, the hero, the lost child, and family clown or mascot.[9] I think that Sam, Ben, and Ally each took on more than one or maybe they changed roles as they oscillated between being at the centre of the issues and being the sibling of another with issues. Sydney was fairly consistent in the role of the "lost child," described as shy, withdrawn, and sometimes invisible. They don't seek or get much attention. They put off making decisions and choose to spend time on solitary activities as a way to cope with the chaos of the home.

At AARC, siblings were given the opportunity to relate to each other in their challenges of living with an addict. My understanding today is that, in general, there's a lot of resentment and anger among kids who've watched their parents respond to constant chaos created by their siblings. Those feelings can be directed at the parents, the siblings, or everyone. Jealousy, frustration, and even some shame are added to the mix when a child's needs are ignored or diminished. Even in chatting with Sydney today, she expresses that she had needs but at the same time, diminishes them and feels almost silly for having feelings about them. This breaks my heart. I hope that someday she allows me to help her find effective counselling to process any feelings that linger. It would be the least I could do.

As we neared the end of treatment at AARC, I learned that it was not just actual chaos that interfered with my ability to parent Sydney—it was also the fear of chaos. I spent so much time in frantic efforts to manage the scariest things in our home that I just felt grateful that Sydney was in her room, not sneaking out, not trying to kill herself, not harming herself, and not demanding energy that I just didn't have. I convinced myself that she was "fine," growing up okay, doing well in school, eating, sleeping, etc. and that that was sufficient. It breaks my heart to think about it today. I let fear of a dire future for the other three kids take over my entire focus. In hindsight, here are a few things I'd have done differently:

- I'd have looked after myself better so that I could've been more present with Sydney. I wish I'd gotten help for each of us.
- I'd have taken time to go for walks or drives with her, allowing her the space to share with me what was going on in her life—just time together away from drama and distractions.
- I'd have taken the time to share with her how the chaos felt for me so she could see me as human, which would've maybe given her permission to be more open about how she was doing.

Endnotes

9   https://www.outofthestorm.website/dysfunctional-family-roles
https://alcoholselfhelpnews.wordpress.com/2007/04/06/alcoholic-family-roles/

CHAPTER TWENTY-ONE

Late in the summer of 2014, I sat in Joan's office for a one-on-one meeting. I'd come to look forward to these meetings and I often walked away with a new insight. On this day we talked about addiction as a lifelong issue and how to reengage with the boys when they finished the program.

Steve and I felt like this was a very big and unknown stage of recovery. We'd come from a place where our kids were using drugs and alcohol and our homes were in chaos. Even though the treatment was delivered in stages with increasing independence for the kids and even though it incorporated lots of practice having our kids home with us, we were entering into unchartered territory. Our kids would no longer be "accountable" to the counsellors at AARC and we'd all be without the structure we'd been living with for almost a year.

Joan asked me if I was anxious or fearful of the transition, and I responded that yes, I was: I just wanted to know what rules we should have in place for post-treatment. What was reasonable? What could and should we expect? She didn't allude to or disclose any concrete rules for the boys but instead kept redirecting me to talk about how I might conduct myself! Our tendency as mothers, she told me, is to revert back to our pre-treatment behaviours, which are driven by fear. We'd be tempted to micromanage our kids' recovery and obsess about whether or not they were doing what they needed to do once they got home. She was right. I reflected on how we'd managed Ben's discharge from his first treatment in Quebec—the sobriety contract and the random drug testing and counselling we'd set up. And again, looking at leaving AARC, I was already anxious to know how to ensure Sam and Ben did what they needed to do. I was focused on their behaviour, not my own!

Part of Joan's job was to help parents stop micromanaging behaviours and learn to let go. For years prior, I'd been confused about the difference between "letting go" and "giving up on my kids." What would letting go look like for a healthy person? How would I behave when I was looking after myself and letting the kids do the same?

Throughout our time in AARC, we learned about the chronic and progressive nature of addictions. All of the staff who worked with the kids were in some form of recovery and they offered invaluable insight into how an addicted person thinks (or doesn't think, in some cases), as well as reminders that addiction lasts forever.

Whenever we were asked to consider the illness alongside the fact that we couldn't control our children's use or recovery, I felt anxious. I'd recall very quickly the frustration, anger, and futility of all my efforts over the past five years. It dawned on me that I really couldn't control any of it. I couldn't prevent my child using or dying, nor could I ensure my child's victory over addiction. It truly was up to them. It was their journey and, as one counsellor reminded me, I needed to "Let them own their failures as well as their victories." But this took lots of practice.

On this day with Joan, I was describing my fears that Sam would hurt himself again. He still seemed to get hopeless and reckless very quickly. With his history of self-harming and suicide attempts, this presented a terrifying combination. Since his diagnosis of BPD, I'd come to understand that his emotions were volatile. But I was no less frightened when I thought about him getting hurt or dying.

I reflected on the pattern I'd noticed in Sam before AARC. I took myself back to those times when everyone was getting ready for bed and he'd start drinking coffee. As I was turning out lights, collecting laundry, and loading the dishwasher, he was putting another pod in the Keurig and heaping teaspoons of sugar into a mug. He was clearly gearing up for an evening of being wide awake. On those nights, he'd seem excitable and a little loud. I'd later describe this as sub-manic behaviour. He wasn't in school and wasn't working. He was trying to recover from his psychotic break and doctors recommended he stay on a regular routine. Staying up all night was a trigger for psychosis. And without the looming deadline of a morning alarm for work or school, a reasonable bedtime was difficult to enforce.

As I watched him pour late-night coffees, I'd hold my breath. I'd find myself not looking at him and yet frantically trying to think of some magical thing to motivate him to go to bed and get some sleep. I'd try not to worry about falling asleep upstairs while my sick son hallucinated in the basement, high on caffeine. Then I'd try not to think about the last time he decided to get some beer and just sat and drank alone all night. It was terrifying to consider how quickly he could escalate to a suicide attempt. When his busy mind started to race, he didn't feel good. And then he would say he couldn't see a future for himself, that life was hopeless, and he might as well end the suffering.

I'd invariably say something before finally heading upstairs. One time it was, "You should not drink that. You need to go to bed." Another time, "Please don't drink coffee, Sam. You need your sleep and so do we." Or maybe, "Sam, what are you thinking? The doctor said you need to sleep at night. You'll never get better if you don't get on a regular schedule and look after yourself." Not surprisingly, none of this was effective. He didn't sleep and neither did I.

I told Joan this. I related how concerned I was for Sam's health post-treatment. "What are you afraid of?" she asked.

I considered the question. "I am afraid he will have another psychotic break."

"What will happen if he has another psychotic break?"

I looked at the floor and reflected that if he had another break, he might suffer permanent brain damage or hurt himself or someone else.

"What would that mean for you?" Joan asked.

I felt as though a movie was quickly playing in front of me. I saw and felt my own distress when Sam was hospitalized for his first psychotic break, my shock and disbelief that my brilliant little boy was no longer able to see what was real and what was not. I remembered how he shuffled around the psychiatric ward in a hospital gown and slippers, sedated on antipsychotics. I felt that fear acutely again. What if this was a permanent state? What might this mean for us as a family? Would Sam be permanently dependent on us? Or would he become one of those people we saw downtown talking out loud to himself as he wandered the streets?

I got anxious as I imagined how that would feel. And there it was. My own pain! It was the fear of my own pain that was driving me to step in when Sam began to drink a pot of coffee at 9:00 p.m. If he wasn't okay, ultimately, my fear was that *I* wouldn't be okay. And the understanding that I was avoiding my own pain was both startling and, eventually, freeing.

While I couldn't control someone else, I could learn to manage my own feelings and take strategies to deal with my own pain. Living in Sam's pain had been excruciating. Only he could manage his behaviours to handle it. If I let myself ride that wave with him, I became a victim to his behaviours. And then I'd act out, trying to make him change. But living with and learning to manage my own pain seemed doable. I just had to separate mine from his. I had choices where and how I spent my energy. I could spend it focusing on the fear of an unknown future beyond my control or I could spend it in the present, noticing and appreciating things that brought me joy.

There's a saying I've heard that sums this up: "Fear does not spare you tomorrow's pain, but it does rob you of today's joy." My fear of the boys' future was robbing me of my joy in the present—it kept me from being able to focus on Sydney, for example, and all the other things that were going well in our family and in my life.

Learning to ride your own roller coaster, as opposed to riding on someone else's emotional roller coaster, takes practice. Becoming aware of how you feel in any given moment is the first step. When you notice negative feelings, notice where you feel it in your body. Step away and take some deep breaths. Acknowledge the feeling, thank it for showing up and for leaving. When someone else is struggling with negative feelings, remind yourself that their pain is theirs and that you don't need to live in it. You can leave, distance yourself, focus on what you need—and then do what you can do to return to feeling yourself.

Reflective Questions:

- Are you spending time focusing on what's going well? What could you celebrate in the present?
- Are there other people in your life who deserve and need as much attention as those who aren't doing well?
- What choices are you making regarding how you spend your limited energy?

CHAPTER TWENTY-TWO

When I worked for Alberta Health Services, I'd had a good benefits program and I took full advantage of it, believing I was looking after myself. I spent a fair amount on expensive haircuts and I'd use my benefits for monthly massages. I got my nails done regularly too. When I visited my doctor back in the fall of 2012 to talk about my stress at work and home, he told me self-care was important for my health. I looked at him and frowned. "Yes," I thought, "I know." I thought it was obvious that I didn't scrimp; I'd spent a lot of money and thought I was doing all I could to take care of myself. For a time, I went to the gym and exercised before or after work. For a few years, we even did family karate! I thought I had it all looked after. And yet, I didn't feel good. And I certainly didn't sleep well at night.

I vividly remember going for monthly massages and lying on the table, my mind racing. I'd be ruminating, obsessing over what had happened at work or at home, and what might happen next. "I can't believe she said that to me today—what did she mean?" "I wish I'd done x, y, or z differently— maybe I can go back and fix it." "I should've said *this* to him today. Darn it, next time I'll be ready." I'd review conversations in my head, compulsively considering what I could've done better, and how I might change or alter my approach in any given situation to ensure the outcomes I wanted. Then

I'd catch myself and think, "Stop thinking, Maureen. Notice the massage. Feel it. You love massages. Tomorrow you'll wish you were here. Try to enjoy it today." This would slow my hamster wheel of a brain for a moment or two but it wouldn't be long before I was right back into my thinking again.

I worked obsessively and I *thought* obsessively about my kids and work. I couldn't slow down or take a break from all the planning and coordinating, all in an effort to control things beyond my reach: other people.

There were years when my thoughts would keep me up at night and I'd spend time watching the clock tick through the minutes and hours in the dark. I'd review over and over the past days, weeks, and months looking for instances where I'd messed up. Then my mind would race to the future, imagining terrible and tragic outcomes for the kids. I speculated about various actions I could take and conversations I could have in an effort to avoid those outcomes. As I did this, I'd feel my heart race, knowing that I was missing valuable sleep and that I'd be tired again the next day. But I felt unable to break these patterns.

I lived each moment in either the past or the future. Never in the present. The past was all about shame and regret, and the future was all about fear. I had no idea how to be still, how to get in touch with myself, and how to handle what I was feeling. And I certainly didn't relate that to self-care. Another saying comes to mind here: "We crucify ourselves between two thieves: regret for yesterday and fear of tomorrow." *Crucify* is a good word. It's like constant torture. And again, I didn't know that my busy mind was a huge part of not knowing how to look after myself in a meaningful or enduring way.

A couple of years later, I had learned some self-care while in the AARC program. I had learned to sleep when I was tired, and I had learned to stop focusing on others and instead get in touch with how I was feeling. But by late 2014, my accumulated fatigue was challenging me and my patience. The kids were well resourced and knew what they needed to do to look after themselves. By contrast, I felt like I was at the beginning of the same journey. What resources did I need? How would I look after myself? I set up a routine of waking naturally, having a light breakfast, taking a short walk with Chloe, my Bernese mountain dog, doing some light work, and then possibly napping if I felt tired. I hated the fatigue. I felt betrayed by my body.

By spring of 2015, I found that some days I felt like I had more energy and I'd think, "Finally, I'm coming out of it," only to be blindsided the next day by a blanket of fatigue. I was growing increasingly impatient with myself.

I formed an entrepreneurial support and accountability group with some women I'd met at various networking events and we got together in my home about once a month. One of the women, Erin, was the founder of Centrivity, a coaching practice focusing on change and transformation. She had a product that she wanted to test with the group. Erin is a petite, dynamic blonde in her thirties with a big smile. She's a strong, gentle, independent, and beautiful entrepreneur who's dedicated herself to being an incredible mom and an advocate for women, our potential for deeper relationships, and for bringing out the absolute best in those she interacts with. I would describe her, in short, as a warrior for female empowerment.

I volunteered to be a sample coaching client, part of which involved standing up to talk to Erin and the group about my self-evaluation of my own health. My satisfaction level regarding my physical health was low because of my fatigue and that spilled over into my satisfaction with my work. As Erin coached me in front of the group, I struggled to dig deep and answer her questions—my feelings were intense and I could feel tears welling up as I talked about what it was like to be so low on energy. She asked me about the intensity of those feelings and as I stood there trying to answer, I began crying openly. I was so embarrassed. What was my problem? I could sense from Erin and the group a desire for me to have self-compassion. I could see empathy on their faces and hear the subtext to their questions, which was that I needed to let go of whatever was blocking my ability to accept where I was.

As we dug deeper, it clicked: I felt *unproductive*. And being unproductive was *lazy*. It hurt to even say the words. Productivity was yet another layer of my identity as a strong and capable woman and it was peeling away. That wasn't fair! I'd felt broken for so long—for *years*—and here I was, working hard to be open to a new way of being a woman, a mother, and a wife. I'd changed so much. I'd let go of so much. And now, I was being stripped once again of another layer of an identity I'd worked hard to build—that of a hardworking professional and budding entrepreneur.

My intense fear was that this unproductiveness was going to become a permanent state, not just a temporary frustration and inconvenience. It felt like a crisis of identity. I'd been fighting the feeling that I was proving my father right—I really was a lazy quitter. And I would be unworthy, as I had always feared, of love and acceptance. Right there in front of the group, I sobbed. How deep did these childhood messages go? They'd impacted everything in my life, from my behaviour to my relationships. It was that old, unwelcome message from so long ago keeping me stuck.

Erin gently invited me to consider another perspective. She asked me what I would tell a cherished friend about self-care. And that's when it came to me, like a strong ocean wave, almost like I might get knocked off my feet—self-care *is* productive. If I could learn to really believe this, it could be a game changer.

All my life, that old fear of being lazy and unproductive had gotten in the way of my truly taking care of myself. I'd spent countless hours, days, weeks, and months chasing my kids, nagging, pushing, and pleading with them to do what they needed to look after themselves. I'd been preaching to them that they needed to learn how to make looking after themselves a priority. I could see clearly that, for them, it was the first step in finding happiness and it wasn't a waste of time. In fact, I told them, if you don't make looking after yourself a priority, everything else will fall apart. And it was true. Now I needed to realize it was true for me too.

After that meeting, over the weeks, and then years that followed, I'd be reminded of this again and again. And I'd be struck by the parallels between what I was experiencing and what my kids were learning. In fact, as I've learned to look after myself, so have they. The more I focus on my own care, the better they (and I) do!

Reflective Questions:
- Do you take your own advice?
- Are you asking your loved one to take actions to look after themselves that you're not taking for yourself?
- How do you role model what you're asking your kids or loved ones to do?

CHAPTER TWENTY-THREE

In 2016, I had an interesting discussion about BPD with a friend. She had had experience working with marginalized women in British Columbia who'd been the victims of domestic violence. She'd done some research with these women and argued that a diagnosis of BPD could not only be a detriment to their lives moving forward but that it might also be invalid. She said that in her opinion, these women had developed very natural responses to very abnormal conditions and that the label of BPD in general was unfair, led to caregiver bias, and sometimes even acted as a barrier to programs that people needed because of the reputation that BPD people were "difficult" to deal with.

I was floored to hear the validity of the diagnosis itself challenged. I was also alarmed that she had seen some discrimination against people with the diagnosis—that people had been, in her words, dismissed by providers. I suddenly worried for my own kids. Would they encounter the same bias? This set me on the path of an investigation about what was going on in the broader world of psychology and counselling, in the world beyond my own experience.

My own experience was that getting the diagnosis for Sam and Ally hadn't just pointed us to effective treatment, it had also led to a better understanding of what drove their behaviours. Further, I was so grateful that although the protocol is not to give an official diagnosis before 18 years of age, Ally's doctor had seen that she met the criteria at 15. This allowed her to start treatment earlier, which has been proven to have better outcomes. I've since chatted with other mothers of kids with BPD and frustration is common regarding the paradox that professionals can be reluctant to provide this diagnosis for those under 18, even though the treatment is considered the most effective before 18.

I decided to call a psychologist friend who was also an educator of other mental health professionals and ask for his perspective. He confirmed that there was bias, stating that BPD was an attachment disorder based in early childhood trauma and a failure to attach to the mother. I didn't appreciate the mother-blaming that has been going on in the mental health field for centuries. A diagnosis of BPD has links to environment but interestingly, it's also linked to genetics, brain structure, and chemical issues, as well as hereditary conditions.[10] I spoke to Donna Hughes, the executive and clinical director of Inner Solutions. She confirmed that there were old biases in the medical community, based on old research. She said the community was in desperate need of more studies and a better understanding of the disorder's pathophysiology. I concluded that while the diagnosis may be a catch-all label used to describe difficult-to-treat patients, for others it is a legitimate and very helpful diagnosis that lends itself to helpful treatment.[11]

My hope is that the medical community stays on top of current information, as opposed to relying on out-of-date information released in the first DSM and carried without challenge into current editions. Donna mentioned Sashbear, a nonprofit group in Ontario supporting some research that showed biological differences in the brain physiology of patients with BPD. In Sashbear, and in Lynn Courey its founder, I discovered a mutual passion for education and advocacy and we decided to offer their Family Connections program here in Calgary. Space was donated by Inner Solutions and Lynn and a colleague came to Calgary to facilitate. It was through this program that I learned the most about BPD and how to best support my kids.

One of my biggest lessons from the Family Connections Program was learning the importance of validation. Validation can be described as the skill used to communicate acceptance and understanding of the feelings a person in expressing. It's closely tied to empathy and compassion, as it requires us to connect to the feeling behind what someone is saying. First, we need to identify another person's feeling, then find that feeling in ourselves, and then express to the other that we can identify with their feelings. This lets people know they're not alone. The connection to another person through acknowledgement and acceptance of their emotion lets people know that they're seen, heard, and accepted.

This hadn't been my approach with most people over the years. In fact, whenever anyone told me told about a difficulty they were experiencing, I'd try to help them see "the bright side" or another perspective. For example, when Ally was in primary school, she occasionally came home lamenting that she didn't have any friends. I'd quickly respond with, "That's not true, Ally. You do have friends! What about your playdate with so-and-so last weekend?" Instead of cheering her up, my response left her feeling invalidated and more alone. Ally didn't need an objective truth or help seeing the inaccuracies in her story. She needed to be acknowledged for her loneliness. She didn't need a discussion about the validity of her story; she needed a discussion that included the validity of her feelings. All feelings are valid, even when the story we create to justify them isn't true or doesn't make sense. This is an important distinction: when we are using validation skills for emotion, we're validating the feelings, not the facts of the story.

For years and years, my responses had been invalidating and I'd inadvertently driven a wedge into my relationships. This new approach I was taught created stronger relationships and trust, and I wanted both of those things with my kids. With practice, it's become almost second nature.

I also learned through experience that it's much easier to validate effectively if you're looking after yourself and it's very tough to do when you feel taxed and overextended. Just one more reason to focus on self-care! As I got better at validation, I saw the tremendous impact it had on Ally and her recovery from self-harm.

One evening, I opened Ally's bedroom door to once again find her cutting her arms. Her face told me she expected the usual admonition and anger. Instead, I considered how she must be feeling—possibly frustrated, sad, anxious, and ashamed, and I tapped into those same feelings in myself. I told her that I loved her and was sorry that she was struggling. I said, "It must be so difficult to deal with how you're feeling, Ally," and then I crawled into bed and snuggled with her. I remember her crying and my heart hurting as I felt her sadness. I let her know that I believed in her and her ability to get better and that slips were bound to happen. It was another moment of grace for me, connecting with her in compassion and love instead of my usual anger, fear, and frustration.

I felt so close to her that night. I felt so much better equipped to be her mom, to just love and accept her. Gone was the old panic, fear, and pressure that had made me so reactive the year before. I had a choice in how I responded and I didn't feel the compulsion to manage her. I was feeling more grateful. I'd been practicing self-care and I'd learned validation skills. As I had learned to accept myself, I had also learned to accept others. All of this led to my ability to demonstrate compassion.

I was finally able to support Ally instead of adding to her shame and misery. We have talked recently about that night as a turning point in our relationship. Today, Ally describes her self-harm years as being desperately lonely for her. She talks about a feeling of emptiness, of feeling bad and not knowing it was abnormal or temporary. She says she needed help but didn't know how to ask for it. She says she needed someone who she felt was on her side, instead of someone judging her and getting angry when she self-harmed.

This explains why, when I could finally accept her, accept myself, and change my behaviour to include validating and expressing my love for her, our relationship and her ability to stay healthy seemed to shift as well. As I got healthier, compassion and acceptance got easier. As I became more accepting that my kids were experiencing pain that wasn't mine to take away, I seemed to get healthier. I could support them, validate them, and empathize with their struggle but I couldn't take it away and I couldn't control the outcome. My efforts to do so had failed repeatedly, damaged my relationships, and left me depleted, sad, frustrated, and frantic.

There's a belief that if we fix the "sick" person, all will be well. I believed it too. And I was shocked to discover that the fixing started with me.

Reflective Questions:
- If you could shift to one degree more acceptance of where others are today, how would that impact your relationship?
- What parallels are there between your self-acceptance and your acceptance of others?

- What would be a benefit of becoming more accepting?
- What is holding you back?

Endnotes

10   https://www.mayoclinic.org/diseases-conditions/borderline-personality-disorder/symp-toms-causes/syc-20370237

11   https://www.ncbi.nlm.nih.gov/pmc/articles/PMC4579503/

https://apalacheecenter.org/2017/12/05/mental-health-matters-borderline-personality-disor-der-stigmatization/

CHAPTER TWENTY-FOUR

And that brings us to that summer day in 2016. As you learned at the beginning of my story, my phone rang. And as you also know, it was Sam. He sounded flat. He said he was in an emergency ward but he was okay. Paramedics had taken him there after a suicide attempt the night before. My heart ached as I listened to his palpable sadness, as he tried to reassure me he was okay. I stopped what I was doing and headed to the hospital.

As I passed lots of other patients and visitors on the way to Sam, it occurred to me that some of them had likely overheard the staff in their efforts to treat Sam for his overdose. They may have overheard his various consciousness checks, conversations about how he was found, his vitals, and all the efforts to get a history on this patient. In years past, I would have felt compelled to try to control and manage the impression we made. I'd have been embarrassed at all this being overheard. But this time, I was only peripherally aware of being observed by the staff as I came in, sat next to him, took his hand, and hugged him hello.

We were separated from the rest of the ward by a thin curtain that opened at the corners. I told him I was glad that he was still alive and with us. Initially, he said he was glad, too, but then he said, actually, no, he wasn't. He wished he was dead. That was a punch to the gut. I felt winded. My breath was shallow and my heart felt squeezed as I looked at my little boy on the stretcher. He looked like he wanted to crawl out of his own skin as he lay there with an IV in his arm and specks of dirt and vomit on his shirt and pants. I swear I could feel his pain. It was so deep, so raw, and so dark. It occurred to me in that moment that if I felt that pain all the time, I'd want to die too.

In the past, I had been acutely aware of how I presented as a professional and as a mother when I was accompanying my kids to appointments. As our lives became increasingly chaotic it had become increasingly important to me to appear as though I had it all together.

But in this moment, I was concerned with Sam and how sad and tortured he was to be driven to such ends. There may've been others looking at me, wondering how my mothering had resulted in the chaos my son was experiencing. They may have judged my clothes, my hair, my vocabulary, or anything else to be an indication of some failing that I had as a nurturer, protector, and mother. They may've concluded that I had failed to bond with my kid or subjected him to some kind of abuse or neglect. After all, something had led to that day, with my son on a stretcher after an overdose and me there next to him, clearly unable to reverse whatever damage had been done. It would've been human nature for them to look for clues.

This wouldn't be Sam's last attempt at suicide. He tried a total of nine times between 2012 and the rest of 2016, and some of them were very, very close calls. He had many angels who found him, called police and ambulances, and helped resuscitate and support him. I'm eternally grateful for each and every one. And during this time, I learned to let go even more, to surrender and trust. There are plenty of people who die by suicide, who are not found in time. We know a few. And the feelings I had each time Sam survived were incredible relief and gratitude mixed with sadness and a sense of resignation that what is meant to be will be—that we do all we can and then we have to let go of the outcome. My belief today is that Sam was meant to live. He has had a journey that's included many hopeless days, attempts to die—and learning how to climb out of that dark pit of despair so he could live.

I don't believe that a parent gets to this place of acceptance until they have to. Only after repeated instances proving that I could not control my child's fate did I finally come to accept it. For me, it has been a matter of faith. Today, I choose to have faith that things go the way they're meant to.

It brings me a sense of peace to do all that I can to help my children and then to let go of whatever happens next.

Reflective Questions:

- In which circumstances are you hanging on to the belief that you have the power to control another person?
- Can you articulate the difference between influence and control?
- What evidence do you have that your efforts to control are effective or ineffective?
- How would letting go of that belief change your story about yourself?

CHAPTER TWENTY-FIVE

In the years since AARC, I've been fascinated with the topic of resilience, especially when it comes to understanding addiction and mental health issues. We were taught the disease model of addiction at AARC but I wanted more.

Why would this disease manifest in some people and not others? Would a predisposition for it show up in all the kids of a given family, or none? How does nature versus nurture play out with mental health and addictions? Both Steve and I have a family history of addiction so why didn't it show up in all of our kids? And if it's a "nurture" issue, why would only some of our kids have issues but not all of them? Furthermore, how do you reconcile my own traumatic childhood with my apparent lack of addictions? My own kids grew up in a home that I would've loved to have been raised in but they struggle with mental health and addictions. How does all this fit together?

A few years ago, I started seeing memes on Facebook quoting Gabor Maté, a physician and author who works with one of the roughest and most heavily drug-addicted populations in Canada, in Vancouver's downtown east side. The posts cited the link between childhood trauma and addiction. I read things like, "Did you know? There is a stronger link between childhood trauma and addiction than there is between obesity and diabetes." I'd open up social media in the morning and this would be in my face. And I was increasingly sensitive to over-simplifications and assumptions regarding causes of mental health and addictions.

My frustration mounted as I once again fought the implied judgement that my kids had suffered abuse and trauma in our home. It seemed as though Maté was popularizing the idea that if you had an addict in your family, there must have been some kind of abuse.

There are *links* between abuse and trauma and addiction,[12] but that does not mean that all addicted people have experienced abuse. The causes of addiction are complex and what we know so far is that there are many overlapping factors between a person's biology, their mental health, their family history, and their childhood experiences that can have an influence on addiction and vice versa.

For example, a maternal history of stress, especially during pregnancy, can influence the formation of certain genetic receptors in the brain of a child, which in turn can have some influence on how a child processes stress. This, in turn, can influence that person's susceptibility to addiction.[13] Also, the child in utero experiences the same physiological responses to the maternal stress hormones as the mother, effectively feeling the stress with her.[14]

Take my own experience as a child and my ensuing lack of addiction to alcohol or drugs. Combined with my knowledge of our family home and the evidence I had that my own kids were indeed struggling with addiction to drugs and alcohol, it's apparent that there's more than a simple straight line going from one point called "Childhood Trauma" to another point called "Addiction."

I believe that oversimplification leads to assumptions, which in turn leads to unspoken judgements and then, of course, shame and isolation. I'd been fighting that shame since the morning we sent Ben off to his first treatment in Quebec. I felt like I was being judged as a crappy mother and for years it felt like it was confirming my worst fears—that maybe I was. But I'd begun to accept that I didn't cause my kids' addictions. And there was no "trauma" as I had defined it (as synonymous with abuse) that caused it either.

A short time later, I saw the meme, yet again, on Facebook. I impulsively commented, "What a load of bullshit" and hit ENTER. I took a deep breath and felt momentarily vindicated. And then I waited. The woman who'd posted the meme read my comment shortly afterward and was kind enough to reach out and ask me about it. I replied, a little more calmly, that I took offence at the implied causal link, which wasn't always true and that I believed it invited judgement that could in turn contribute to families' isolation for fear of being judged. She very kindly took the post down.

I have a better understanding of Gabor Maté's message today and no longer have the same reaction to the link between trauma and addiction. My understanding today is that when he uses the word trauma, he is not talking about *what* happened but rather *how* a person internalizes what happened or what didn't happen as a child. I continue to look into the concepts of epigenetics and inherited family trauma and how to break the cycle and heal. But that journey really began with my kids and my drive to understand why they were struggling.

There were mutterings at this time that marijuana was going to be legalized in Canada and there was much debate, many advocates and many detractors. AARC held an educational forum called Marijuana and the Teenage Brain. I decided to attend. I sat in a large, dark presentation room and listened to the consulting psychiatrist present her work with addicts. "Some of us are born orchids," she said, "and some of us are born dandelions." I got goosebumps when she explained that this means that some people are born with so many protective qualities against adversity that they can take root in the crack of a sidewalk and bloom. These are the dandelions, who seem to be able to thrive in even the most adverse conditions—in any type of soil, with any amount of water. Even when pulled out, a bit of root hangs on, the plant regenerates, and eventually blooms. These are the kids who seem to be able to bounce back after facing serious adversity—the ones who are born extra resilient.

And then some of us are orchids who seem to need just the right type of soil, the right type of light, and just the right amount of water. If we're orchids, we need very specific conditions in which to thrive, and if one of the conditions is off, we may struggle to thrive and bloom. These are the kids we hear described as sensitive and who may struggle even if the environment appears to be supportive. These are the kids who I would describe as sometimes not being a good fit with their family of origin, particularly if that family were all made up of dandelions.

This made sense to me, finally. I had been searching for an explanation for my own lived experience. According to this analogy, some people, even at birth, seem more adaptive and better able to take advantage of even a whiff of resilience-building factors. Others can be born into and raised in relatively stable environments, with seemingly every opportunity, and yet they may struggle to thrive.

The lecture opened my eyes to a new way of understanding how things in my family had turned out the way they did. The analogy offered a way of explaining a starting point for what I now believe is a very complex bio-psychosocial process. To this day, it helps put my mind at ease when I'm tempted to look for a cause for my kids' mental health and addiction struggles. I've wrestled with my role in their issues. I've wrestled with feeling responsible for not being the mother they needed, with the belief that my mothering could have changed things. I no longer believe in any simple, straight line linking an event or a gene to how a person's life plays out. How our genes and our environment mesh together over time is individual and unpredictable. It cannot be simplified to any one event or trait.

I see almost everything on a spectrum now, and I use a spectrum model when I'm trying to explain mental health, addictions, and resilience. It's my theory that everyone experiences every diagnosable issue to some degree. It may not be enough to be a problem or need a diagnosis or support but it's there.

First, picture every disorder as a spectrum on a scale from one to 10 (one being not expressed, and 10 being fully expressed). Then recognize that we're all born at a spot on each scale. For example, I could be born a three on the attention deficit disorder scale, a seven on the depression scale, a five on the anxiety scale, and so on. Then as I go through my life, I experience things in such a way that can move my place on the scale down towards a one or up towards a 10. Those events are when the gene is "turned on" and expressed. This is when we have a problem that's interfering with our lives and requires support.

In March 2016, Sam was once again in treatment at AARC and Steve and I were supporting him through the six- to eight-week refresher program. We were once again sitting in AARC's large community room with a group of other parents. We listened to one of the clinicians talk about her formative experiences from childhood. Sometimes AARC's clinicians would share their own addiction experiences and insights. I always sat up a little straighter and listened more intently when they did.

On this evening, the clinical lead told us about an experience in early kindergarten, when her teacher put a question to the class and, in her excitement, she blurted out the answer. She was pleased with herself and expected the teacher would be too. Instead, the teacher said, "When we want to speak, we raise our hand first and wait to be called on." This situation had occurred some 30 years prior but she recounted it like it was yesterday. As she told the story, she used her arms and facial expressions as though she were painting a picture, the scene still colourfully vivid after so much time. She recounted her overwhelming shame and embarrassment, feelings she ended up dealing with years later in recovery. I was deeply moved listening to her. I felt enormous empathy and recalled my own experiences with shame and embarrassment.

At the same time, I was completely struck with how benign that situation would have been for many of the kids in that kindergarten room. Her teacher hadn't done anything unusual. Quite the opposite; that sort of reprimand occurs in classrooms everywhere across the country and likely with some frequency. It may well have happened to me, or my own classmates, though I have no recollection of a specific incident. I was moved to consider how each situation strikes each of us differently, sometimes in very profound ways that we may not even be aware of, even as a witness. A few months later, I'd be reminded of this same concept by my own son.

Ben had met a girl, Ashlly, and about two months after meeting and dating, they discovered that Ashlly was pregnant with Ben's baby. Nine months later, in March of 2016, Athena was born. Ben had been struggling with using throughout the pregnancy and things escalated shortly after Athena was born. He admitted himself to a residential treatment at Recovery Acres in Calgary, another 12-Step program, and Ashlly and Athena moved in with Steve and me. One evening, Ben and I were sitting and chatting about a session he had had with a counsellor in which he recounted a story from grade three. He seemed excited by a new revelation as he leaned forward to share his memory of a significant event from his childhood and the impact it had. He told me that at recess he was playing baseball in the schoolyard and he was running to home base. As he slid home, the catcher, a friend of his, banged Ben's head off the base. He told me about the confusion and hurt he experienced and the resulting shame as he internalized his feelings of shame, that he somehow had deserved to have his head slammed into the plate.

As I listened to him, I wondered to myself how many more instances like this my son (and my other kids, for that matter) had experienced. How could I have any real idea? It also occurred to me that perhaps he'd told me when it happened. There's a good chance that even if he'd come home and told me about it, I would've responded in a way that I thought was normalizing and encouraging. Something like, "I'm sure Jimmy didn't mean anything by it."

In the context of the spectrum model, I hear about those formative experiences—the drug treatment counsellor in kindergarten and my son sliding into home base—and believe they were likely significant enough to move the scale on some of their predisposed conditions toward a 10/10, or full expression. Further, I believe that my kids were born orchids and as such were more susceptible to experience difficult situations that I, a dandelion, would not necessarily find as impactful.

As a mother, this helps me understand why I cannot seem to find "the cause" of their struggles. It helps me put to rest the never-ending post-mortem of their childhoods in an effort to find "the thing" that led us to addiction and mental health issues. It helps me put Ben's reading comprehension issues from childhood into perspective and recognize I'm not ever going to figure it all out. Much of what has impacted my kids is beyond my reach, beyond my memory, and may not have even been within my control, ever.

These days, I help other parents cope with the chaos of having addicted children. And I hear the same undercurrent of self-blame when parents give me a history of mental health and addictions in their homes. I hear their strong desire to identify a cause or explanation as to why things have gone the way they have. I get it. I felt the same way.

I was eager to believe that if I just did X, Y, and Z, my kids would grow up happy and healthy and all of our dreams would come true. I wanted cause and effect—some order, by contrast, to the chaotic home I myself had grown up in. As a young parent, I was counting on it. How could I manage my life and the lives of my family if there was no right and wrong way to do things? Anything less than clarity was unacceptable. I see this desire in every parent I work with today too.

Cause and effect gives us a sense of order, a sense of control. And control keeps chaos and chance at bay. As parents we ought to have control over how our kids turn out. Otherwise, what's the point of busting ourselves in an effort to do everything right? Are we effective or ineffective? Can things really be out of our hands?

As for trauma, I've come to think of it as more than just "abuse." I've concluded that there are Big-T traumas and Little-t traumas. Whereas I'd been focusing on Big-T trauma (physical and sexual abuse) when I heard the link between trauma and addictions, I could've considered that Little-t traumas had a role, like those formative experiences we parents don't even know about. With this framework, I could indeed say that my kids experienced trauma.

Further, drug addiction can happen to anyone, whether they've experienced abuse or not.[15]

It makes sense that we parents can't always know exactly how or why our kids develop mental health and addiction issues. It makes *more* sense that one child in a home can thrive while another struggles. It makes *more* sense that some kids have it relatively good and don't do well, while others who seem very challenged do okay. And it helps me to let go of trying to figure everything out, to let go of carrying all the blame—and this letting go helps me to sleep at night. We all do our best, and what happens next, I trust now, is as it needs to be.

Reflective Questions:
- Do you think you know the cause of your loved one's struggles?
- What would change if you let go of the story you have about what caused their struggles?
- How do you believe knowledge of the cause of their struggles will benefit you or them?
- How could your desire to understand the cause of your loved one's issues impact you and those you love?

Endnotes

12   https://www.ncbi.nlm.nih.gov/pmc/articles/PMC3051362/

13   https://www.drugabuse.gov/publications/research-reports/common-comorbidities-substance-use-disorders/why-there-comorbidity-between-substance-use-disorders-mental-illnesses

14   Wolynn, Mark. It Didn't Start With You: How Inherited Family Trauma Shapes Who We Are and How to End the Cycle. Penguin Life, 2017.

15   https://teens.drugabuse.gov/videos/anyone-can-become-addicted-drugs

CHAPTER TWENTY-SIX

In 2002, I was teaching Nursing in an Ontario hospital. I was walking down a hospital corridor with my 15 students, thinking about the patient we were about to check in on, when—bang! I was back in my childhood home, experiencing feelings of frustration and being trapped as a wave of nausea hit me. I was no longer an adult in a hospital with 15 students trailing me, I was a child again, envisioning a place I didn't want to be and grappling with sensations that felt at once familiar and like a distant memory. "This is it," I thought, "I am officially losing my mind."

I promptly booked an appointment with a local counsellor to deal with it and had about four appointments before I felt like I was back on track. This was the most vivid and intrusive flashback I had ever had. My childhood memories and feelings came uninvited to me to a lesser degree over the years, and I knew that at some point I'd have to go beyond the few appointments I'd had in order to really dig into it.

Nearly 15 years later, a friend described her experience with eye movement desensitization and reprocessing (EMDR) therapy. She told me the treatment is designed to deal with post-traumatic stress disorder and effectively rewires the brain to remove emotional responses to traumatic memories. She described the process and her results, which sounded interesting and appealing. I'd done various talk therapies over the years and while I always gained new insights, I really had trouble letting go of my childhood trauma.

There are studies that support the effectiveness of EMDR therapy and a growing number of practitioners who use it. But there are also naysayers who dispute that it has any more efficacy than traditional cognitive behavioural therapy. I can only convey my own experience.

The EMDR psychologist I was referred to described what would happen in our sessions. She said that I would be asked to visually track an object travelling laterally in front of me. Left to right, right to left, over and over again. While this was going on, I would be asked a set of questions about experiences and my feelings associated with them and then also be challenged to consider my beliefs about myself and the world that may have resulted from those experiences. I would then be asked to consider what I would *like* to feel and believe in the context of those memories as well as describe physical sensations that I had during the process. If the therapy worked, the result would be that I would no longer carry the emotional weight of past trauma. I would remember incidents but they would not have the same emotional impact. It sounded incredibly freeing and worth a try!

As I sat in one of my first sessions in a comfortable chair in a Calgary high-rise, the psychologist began by asking me to create a safe place or a set of thoughts I could use to bring me a sense of comfort, peace, and safety in the event that the therapy caused me distress. I began to consider when, where, and with whom I felt comfort, peace, and safety. My most vivid and immediate thoughts were when I was walking alone with my dog, Chloe, or hanging out with her in my bedroom. She'd lay her head on me as I read or worked on my computer. I was surprised to find this as one of my safest places. Previously, I'd have said it was home with my family and while I wished that were true, it had been a long time since being with my family had felt peaceful.

EMDR was strange but it worked! After seven sessions, my life felt my own—my body was my own. My memories were intact but I no longer felt flooded with feelings at recalling them. Further, my present-day experiences no longer took me back to painful memories—that link seemed to be severed. Freedom! This freedom has had a huge impact on my life and ability to reclaim my experiences as my own, rather than have them linked to memories and feelings from childhood.

One of the big takeaways for me was the link between emotion and physical sensations. During the therapy, when I felt painful emotions, I was surprised and taken off-guard by sudden pain in my knee or shoulder. The pain moved around a little as I talked and moved my eyes and then finally disappeared. I would never have believed it, had I not experienced it. As a result, I started to notice more links between my mind and my body.

For example, when I felt fear, I would take a few moments and take note of the changes I felt physically: Sweaty palms, my chest rising and falling faster as my heart rate and breathing increased, and even a heaviness in my lower abdomen. I'd been previously somewhat detached from my physical self and had never really taken the time to notice that my body gave me great clues to my feelings about something in my life. It was a new awareness and I found it fascinating to place trust in physical feelings instead of just thoughts.

I started to notice clues that my body gave me about places and people as well. When I found myself feeling joyful in a place or with a person, I'd stop to notice what I was experiencing and where in my body I could feel it. Conversely, when I found myself in a situation that was unpleasant, I'd do the same thing. I learned I feel anxiety and distress very tangibly in my gut, whereas I feel lightness and joy in my solar plexus, just below my sternum. I started avoiding things that caused unpleasant sensations and seeking more pleasant ones.

To that end, I took Chloe on more and more walks—along the ridge overlooking a golf course or into a wildlife reserve—and I began to feel better. Watching my dog live joyfully in the moment on a walk (as dogs do) made me feel the same. I loved this new knowledge and the fact that this feeling was available to me anytime I chose to take her out. If for some reason I felt too tired to go out for long, I made sure to take her for at least 10 minutes. That seemed to be enough to bring some joy into my day. And that's an important thing to note: moments of joy can be enough.

This awareness and these feelings became a good guide for me as I was trying to look after myself. I was still more tired than I wanted to be, and I was working at getting my energy back to more consistent levels. Additionally, answering the question of what would bring me the most joy became an intuitive way to make decisions about the direction of my business. Initially, I was a little skeptical about using this question to make business decisions. I was suspicious that if everyone only did things that brought joy, nothing important would get done. Who would do the hard and unpleasant work? Life would turn into nothing more than a relentless pursuit of pleasurable activities. Society would not survive!

As I reflected further on the joy question, I concluded that tackling hard and unpleasant things also brings me joy. Learning to manage all aspects of my business effectively brings me joy. Overcoming my procrastination and accomplishing a task I find difficult brings me joy. Doing work with purpose brings me joy. Sometimes the answer to the question leads me to the vision of finally getting my taxes done and off my plate. I have realized that for me, the pursuit of joy means the pursuit of a meaningful and productive life in which I am fully me and fully living my values. I feel healthier and more productive when I use my intuition and the pursuit of true joy as a guide.

EMDR was life-changing for me. Not only did it rid me of life-long associations that were intrusive and unwelcome but it started me on the path of learning about how I physically experience emotions, what happens when I don't know how to process them, and the freedom associated with handling them in the moment, as opposed to storing them forever.

Reflective Questions:
- Do you know how and where in your body you experience distress and joy?
- How can you avoid more distress and find more joy?
- What choices do you have about how and with whom you spend your time?
- What recurring pattern continues to interfere with your joy? What support could help you change that pattern?
- What do you need to do before you seek that support?

CHAPTER TWENTY-SEVEN

On New Year's Day 2017, Sydney decided to go for a run. It was cold outside but she wanted to start off on the right foot with her New Year's resolution to get better at running. After she returned home, Steve and I both noticed that one of her eyelids was swollen and we attributed it to a sty, a blocked oil duct in her eyelid.

Sydney had turned 20 the year before. She'd become an excellent makeup artist and she knew how to apply products that I still don't understand to create amazing dramatic effects. One of the undesirable effects was that occasionally her make up would clog a pore and she would get a sty, which would resolve in a couple of days. As she sat across from me in our living room chatting, I noticed that the swelling was getting worse and even seemed to be spreading to her other eye as well. As I pondered this, she began to scratch her belly through her shirt. There was a quiet alarm bell starting to go off in my mind and I called her over to take a look at her skin. Sure enough, there were hives all over her trunk. Between the advancing of the swelling and the sudden appearance of a rash, my heart began to race. I calmly but firmly told her to get in the car—we were heading to the hospital, a 10-minute drive away. As we drove, she became unrecognizable. Her face was swelling quickly but she was still okay—amused at the rapid changes her face was undergoing, she was taking selfies. I was grateful that she didn't feel as panicked as I was beginning to feel. She was having an anaphylactic reaction to something, with no history of allergies!

We pulled up to the curb and I took her inside. As she was being triaged, she began to go into shock; I noticed her responses were lagging and she seemed confused. I advised the triage nurse that she was appearing shocky to me and we quickly wheeled her chair into the emergent area of the department. They started an IV, and adrenaline and other emergency drugs were immediately administered. She responded quickly to the drugs and was transferred to a stretcher to complete her assessment and treatment. The staff surmised that she had developed "cold urticaria," or a life-threatening allergy to the cold.

We were in that emergency room for a few hours while she received treatment, and I could hear a lot of what was going on with the patient on the adjacent stretcher. Sydney was now well-stabilized, and while we sat, I stole a few surreptitious glances next door. I estimated the patient there was in his twenties and unconscious. Periodically, a staff nurse or physician would enter and try to rouse him with no response. I heard them asking each other what he took, estimating how many pills might've been missing from various bottles. I had been an emergency room nurse myself decades prior so I couldn't help trying to piece together snippets of conversation to create a clinical picture of what was happening next door. As I sat there, refamiliarizing myself with the equipment and waiting for Sydney to finish her treatment, I tried half-heartedly giving this man his privacy and instead focused on what I remembered from working in critical care.

But I still heard the nurses talking with social workers about calling his family; apparently, they were on their way. I had the distinct impression that this man had had multiple interactions with the medical system, that he had a mental health or addictions history, and that he clearly wasn't winning the battle to be healthy. Nothing like New Year's Day to precipitate a crisis, I thought. It was hard not to hear bits of his saga and fill in the gaps, even as I was trying to make conversation with my own daughter while she lay there getting medicated.

When I heard a clerk enter and ask if the man's mother and sister could join him, I sat up a little straighter. I heard the door open and someone gasp and inhale sharply, and I leaned over so that I could catch a peek. To my great shame, I recall wondering if the mother would "look like the mother of someone who overdoses." What does that even mean? I was struck with how quickly and easily my mind went to this mother-blaming and judgmental place, even though I'd been in her shoes and had at times felt guarded against others judging me. How could I? I was mortified.

When I thought I was being judged, I got angry and fearful of my own failings as a parent. I was righteous about my and Steve's parental successes when our kids were younger, right up until the day I was forced to realize that mental health and addictions don't discriminate. They show up in families who dedicate themselves to keeping kids busy and productive—in families whose kids are bored and under-resourced. Families in single-parent homes, dual-parent homes, loving homes, neglectful homes, homes with educated professional parents. They show up in stay-at-home-mom homes, warm-home-baked-cookies-after-school homes, latch-key homes, home-schooling homes, and so on. There's no single "type" of home that produces kids who struggle.

And yet, this didn't prevent me from judging or looking to the mother as the "cause." This didn't stop me from gawking at this poor mother in crisis to see what she looked like. I didn't think I would I see the idyllic image of a mom who effortlessly adapts to whatever role is needed within her family, emerging unscathed and fulfilled at the end of each day. I anticipated the stereotypical "terrible mother" who can't manage her time, is overwhelmed, and has lost herself and maybe even one of her kids in the chaos.

What floored me in this moment was that despite what I knew, despite the past six years of my own experience, and the times that I had felt judged myself, I still fell into the very ingrained societal trap of believing in a "good mother" profile that results in well-adjusted, successful children.

Sydney was discharged home with an EpiPen, and I was sent home with lots to think about in terms of judgement and how I used it to keep myself separate.

Today, my reflections on judgement are as follows:

- Judgment is a very human way for us to understand the world, and even though we recognize it's driven by fear, we need to learn to suspend it. To suspend judgment means to recognize when it's happening and consciously withhold it.
- My judgment came from a place of fear and a desire to be separate from that mother and the pain of her life. If I could be separate,

I wouldn't have to empathize and recognize my role in the society that fails to meet the needs of its most vulnerable, thus causing them further pain and suffering.

- This woman deserved my love and support and my unconditional positive regard. Because she was human, she deserved my approaching her with the attitude that she was doing her best and that that was all anyone could ask. No judgment.
- While I'm less guilty of judgment today, I'm not out of the woods when it comes to judging others and myself and playing the comparison game. Better than, and therefore okay; or less than, and consequently ashamed.
- We have more in common with the people around us than not. When I focus on what makes us separate, I can take credit for my own successes and leave others with the pain of their own failures. Both are illusions of separateness.

Remember the saying—*It takes a village?* That concept that it takes many members of a community to raise a child into a happy, healthy, and socially responsible adult? This concept has gone by the wayside in the last few generations of individualistic parenting. Today's mantra is more like: "Only I can discipline or be anything less than a cheerleader for my kids."

As we've become our own children's social, moral, educational, and recreational concierges, case managers, and advocates, we've railed against anyone we've seen as a threat to their successes. More often than not, we peg people as threats if they do anything but cheer for our kids—accordingly, coaches, teachers, and other parents have become the enemy. We snap at them, lash out at them, and call them out publicly or on social media. We believe we have to be actively building our children's self-esteem and providing them with every opportunity possible. We take it all on, becoming solely responsible for managing them and their futures.

As outsiders (anyone who isn't the primary caregiver or mother), we've learned to stay out of each other's business. We run the risk of a mother's wrath if we step in or presume to interfere. We're afraid we'll be seen as out of line, harsh, abusive, or just plain nosy. We've taken the concept of advocacy for our kids too far and the result is sole responsibility, isolation, separation, and a whole new kind of comparison and judgement of ourselves and each other as capable parents. This is especially harmful when you have kids struggling with mental health and addictions.

As parents, it's hard to admit we can't do it all. But how could we possibly offer everything a child needs to grow into a happy, healthy, well-adjusted adult? It's why we have community, why friends matter, and why exposure to complex social situations matters. It's why extended family matters, why school and social groups matter, why individual and team sports matter, why coaches matter, and why teachers matter in the development of healthy kids.

It was hard for me to accept that someone else was more capable and qualified to help my kids with their issues. But it was also a relief. When we take sole responsibility for our kids, we absorb responsibility for actions and outcomes that don't belong to us. When our children aren't thriving, we're not thriving. When our children fail, we believe that we fail too. This is scary and unacceptable. It's why we see parents negotiating their children's marks and team positions with teachers and coaches. We're so enmeshed with our kids that we can't let them fail without feeling we've failed too.

We become our kids' sole support. But I've found we're way too emotionally invested to be effective. Our emotional ties, in combination with our efforts to manage our kids, lead to relationship ruin. They're detriments to the health of both the sick individual and the caregiver in the home.

Let others help. If you're the mom, just be the mom.

Reflective Questions:
- What judgments do you hold that you assume others are holding as well?
- Whose opinion are you conscious of? How does your behaviour change as a result? Tap into your gut reaction to the statement, "What that person thinks of you is none of your business" and journal for 10 minutes about how you're feeling.
- How are your judgments keeping you from being authentic and asking for what you really need?
- What are your beliefs about the parenting of kids who are struggling?
- What supports are you trying to provide that would be better provided by someone else?

CHAPTER TWENTY-EIGHT

Sam has struggled with alcohol and drugs, the emotional ups and downs of his BPD, and more suicide attempts, even as he's tried multiple treatment centres, multiple drug treatment modalities, and multiple behavioural therapies since AARC. He came to understand that the 12-Step program and DBT skills were useful but they weren't enough for him. What eventually rounded out his recovery enough for him to stay sober was a triathlon training group he joined in 2017 called the Terminator Foundation, where he learned that completing extreme sports made him feel capable, accomplished, good about himself, and more emotionally regulated. The activity also creates more dopamine receptors that make him feel really good.

Today, Sam is three years sober and healthier than ever. We've talked a lot about his recovery, what got him sober, and how he's stayed that way. When asked what was behind his decision to finally stop using, he said, "I was sitting alone and drinking in my room and I thought, 'I am so tired of this.' So I stopped." He attributes staying sober to a combination of things that include all the various formal treatments he's participated in and his efforts with Terminator. It hasn't been any one thing. And his getting sober certainly didn't fit with the concept of "hitting bottom." Hitting bottom is the common belief that when addicts finally experience a dramatic enough event, they'll make the decision to turn their lives around. Sam had had plenty of dramatic events that didn't do it. Instead, he made the decision to change on a relatively uneventful evening alone in his room.

I heard something similar when I enrolled in a program offered by a local 12-Step guru. He asked the group what we thought inspired him to go to his first AA meeting, after which he got sober and kept going. We all took turns guessing things like losing a job, almost dying, having a friend die, losing family relationships, or getting arrested. Each time we guessed, he would respond, "That did happen, but no, that didn't do it." After a while, we gave up, and he told us what finally inspired him—a pretty girl invited him out for a coffee. She took him to a meeting. He agreed to go because he thought she was cute and he might get lucky. After all the crises he'd been through, it was something run-of-the-mill that prompted him to attend a meeting for addiction. Essentially, when he was ready, he was ready.

I've heard many stories like this now, stories that tell me it's not necessarily a "crisis" that motivates people to change but a benign event at the right moment. A moment in time in which the person feels ready and the spark for change is there. From the outside, and to non-addicts like me, it makes no sense but it seems to happen more often than I would've thought. This experience isn't universal and that's exactly my point. Nothing is predictable, standard, or universal when it comes to taking a path to recovery. Further, it's not typically "one thing" that keeps people sober—it's a mix.

Recovery isn't one-size-fits-all. People may need a variety of interventions and strategies over the course of years to become well: 12-Step programs, psychiatric care, counselling, skills-based therapies, various harm reduction strategies (including medically supervised strategies that involve medications), and lifestyle changes (fitness groups, yoga, etc.).

I now find myself saying it's best to stay out of my kids' business and let them choose for themselves whether to live in recovery or not. I try not to judge and respect their choices instead. I call this the dignity of choice. This isn't easy to do, and I have to remind myself that what's important to me is my relationship with them. To that end, the last time Ben experienced a relapse in 2019, I sent him a text message while he was using and living on the street to ask if he wanted to meet for a coffee. I didn't intend to take him home or even to tell him what he "should" do to get sober. I just wanted to spend some time with him.

I'm able to contemplate this as an option only because I know that Ben, Sam, and Ally are well resourced, meaning they have the knowledge, understanding, experience, and resources to *choose* a life in recovery and live a life that's healthy. I can only step back after I've ensured they understand what's available to them and how to find it if they choose to. The kids are finally well resourced and know what recovery can feel like.

Stepping back from someone who is ill and letting them have their choices before finding good, appropriate, and effective resources is, in my opinion, unfair. That would constitute giving up on a disadvantaged person. A person who is seriously unwell may have a difficult time finding good, available resources. That's not to say it can't be done but particularly when young people are ill, it isn't fair to expect them to be able to seek help. Young people don't often know what it feels like to live in recovery. They may have no idea how to even hope for something different, let alone seek it out.

Once you find solid resources for your kids, even if they don't fully embrace them, you can work on stepping back and looking after yourself. Only after you find the right resources can you reclaim your role as a loving and supportive parent. Your communication style can change to curious, open, loving, and accepting. And this shift is gift—it's a gift to be able to trust others to provide professional support to your loved one if they choose to take it and it allows you to focus on being positive and supportive without the pressure of trying to manage things, fix them, or be the solution, which often doesn't work and isn't sustainable in this marathon of chronic and progressive illness.

Today, I speak to many parents who have yet to find the right help. They're frustrated because they don't know how or where to find the right resources, and as a result, they lose themselves amid all the fatigue and chaos. They aren't the person or parent they want to be. There's such regret and sadness in the many stories I hear about parents reacting in harsh and sometimes even violent ways to their kids' behaviours. These are all loving parents who want the best for their kids but they haven't yet found the right resources to help them let go of trying to fix things themselves. They want to reclaim the role of being a loving mother or father but they just can't. And in the process, they lose sight of who they are. Like I did, they begin to act in ways that no longer reflect the values they hold. I became sarcastic, snippy, erratic, short-tempered, at times resigned and indifferent. None of those behaviours reflect my values.

The search for the right help sometimes takes time and a willingness to experiment. When people talk about the importance of finding a counsellor who "fits," it's not often clear what that means. To me, it means the right person at the right time. Does their style match what you need? Are they qualified to deal with the issues you're having?

Steve and I sought a lot of help from a number of lovely individuals over the years who were underqualified. These people were easily snowed by our kids' ability to say and do all the right things. We visited run-of-the-mill psychologists who claimed to specialize in families or in youth and they had no idea what they were dealing with. They didn't recognize addiction and they weren't qualified to diagnose a disorder. Even though much of the behaviour had yet to reveal itself when we went to a lot of these people, I still knew we weren't dealing with typical rebelliousness. And yet, we were reassured time and again that we were. The recommendations were typical parenting recommendations—stay consistent, enforce boundaries, and so on. Of course, none of it worked. Our kids weren't typical and their problems weren't either.

Having parented three atypical kids and one who seemed typical (Sydney), I now know that all the standard parenting advice and behaviours work like a charm for healthy kids. Sydney followed the rules we enforced and seemed to have an intrinsic motivation to do well by society's standards. She responded to consequences, approval, and disapproval. She asked permission and accepted our no if we gave it (although we rarely, if ever needed to say "no" to her). Even Ally, after treatment, seemed relatively easy to parent. She, too, asked permission and accepted our restrictions on where she went and who she spent time with. Sam and Ben did not. All that standard parenting advice was ineffective with my kids when they were ill.

In my work today, I come across the parents of very sick and atypical kids; they've been paying and visiting psychologists for years without progress and it aggravates me to hear about it. A typical story goes like this: "My child is defiant and has been since he was three. He exhibited unusual behaviours that were disruptive and socially unacceptable even at a young age. Our family doctor suggested more positive reinforcement and it seemed to have little impact. So we just keep trying and now, as a teenager, he's overwhelmed us. Other problem behaviours have developed and our home is in chaos. He has a counsellor that he agrees to go and see and has for a few years. But nothing seems to get better. We continue to go because it's good for him to have someone he feels comfortable talking to. We don't know what the goal of the treatment is, or if it's working, but we don't know what else to do. Overall, we are fed up. He is not functional. He defies us at every turn. We walk on eggshells."

I know exactly how this person feels. Our boys didn't buy in and get better until we sought treatment from an organization staffed by people close to their own age who'd been through the same program to treat mental health and addictions. These individuals could spot BS a mile away. They weren't inclined to coddle or put up with much. They could be compassionate, empathetic, strong, and straightforward at the same time. The phrase "You can't bullshit a bullshitter" comes to mind.

It's important to note that, as a society, we've learned an awful lot about how to assess and treat mental health disorders. But all things being relative, we're still in the dark ages when it comes to understanding the brain and mind.[16] Diagnosing and treating psychological and mental health issues is still a lot of trial and error. Further, it relies largely on honest disclosure, which can prove to be a challenge for people struggling with shame or a lack of self-awareness.

Consider carefully the goals of your treatment. You want more than just a supportive listener. Sometimes people don't often think of counselling as coming with an articulated outcome or goal, but you can still talk about them and goals are something you can cocreate with your practitioner.

Many of us think that if we find someone for our kids to talk to, they'll suddenly develop insight; maybe another adult will tell them what to do and they'll listen because it's not us! It's important to ask: What will success look like? What's your process? What can we expect? I'd recommend not settling for a simple answer from a therapist, such as, "Your son/daughter will get out of it what they put into it." It's true but you need to dig deeper. It's vital that both parties understand where you're going so you'll know when you get there. Endless talking about *why* you feel the way you do without some strategies (behavioural therapies) may not lend itself to change.

And change is what we're after here, especially with dysfunctional youth and chaotic family homes and dynamics. I recommend you ask questions and choose a skills-based behavioural program with someone who's been through it, or who has experience helping people just like you!

Here are seven questions you can ask any practitioner you're considering:

1. Are you licensed? Who are you licensed with, and is your license active and in good standing? Look for a yes and licensing through a known regulatory body.

2. Where did you get your degree? What type of training or clinical experiences have you had in treating the kinds of problems I'm having or my loved one is having (mood problems, anxiety, sleeping difficulties, etc.)? Look for a known higher-education institution and experience with treating the issues you're having.

3. How many years have you been seeing clients? (I prefer someone with some experience under their belt.)

4. What is/are your area(s) of expertise? (I look for someone with expertise in the area I am struggling with.)

5. What type of treatments do you use? How effective are they in dealing with situations similar to mine? How do you know if treatment is working, and what do you do when it isn't? Look for concrete answers here that resonate with you.

6. How much do you charge? Do you issue receipts so I can claim the cost with my insurance or health plan? Do you have availability in the [mornings, afternoons, evenings, weekends]? When's the earliest date I can see you for our first appointment? Again, look for answers that suit you here.

7. Does your work in therapy tend to be more focused on the past or the present? Do you tend to see people for long-term therapy or for shorter-term therapy? Reflect on what you're looking for and look for answers that are in alignment.

CHAPTER TWENTY-EIGHT

Endnotes

16   https://www.richmond.com/news/modern-psychiatry-still-in-the-dark-ages/article_
c968e31b-db3b-5ce3-a584-ca93298d6ff9.html

CHAPTER TWENTY-NINE

One afternoon in 2019, as I stood at the front of a classroom in an old building named Heritage Hall, the sun streaming through large windows highlighting the older-style trim and brickwork. I was teaching at a local college and my students were adults from a cross section of industries. They reflected on my instructions: "Consider the times in your life in which you've learned the most about who you are and what you're capable of." I was teaching a leadership course for the School of Business, and as is typical of my courses, I waded with them into the realm of human behaviour, mental health, and resilience.

Each participant looked off into the distance or at their desks for a moment and then quickly they put pen to paper to write down these significant times in their lives. When asked to share, one gentleman raised his hand and sat up a little straighter as he recounted a time in which he'd lost his job. He talked about how it seemed as if all the cards were stacked against him, about how initially he felt despair and failure and a very real fear and concern that he'd not be able to support himself or his family. He painted a bleak picture that many of us fear: The loss of purpose and income and the fear of letting those around us down. It was a bleak few months for him and his family. When he couldn't find a job in the same field, he was forced to make a change and look for work in a new field, one with which he wasn't familiar—he felt underqualified and afraid. Today, he describes that loss as a blessing in disguise; it made him stretch and work toward something he didn't know he was capable of. He reinvented himself and proved to himself and the world that he was capable of more than he thought.

I asked him where he thought he might be today had he not been faced with that adversity and been allowed to work through it. He sat back, stared at the ceiling for a moment, and then said that he might feel locked in the belief that he was only good at making a living on one career path. He hadn't been happy in his old line of work but it was all he knew. He'd hit the income ceiling in that job and felt stuck. Today, he makes more money and enjoys his work more than he did in his old role.

I ask this type of question in almost every class I've taught in the past five years. I've yet to find a class in which students couldn't identify a crisis that ultimately made them stronger. Sometimes it even gave them a new purpose.

We reflected as a group on how beneficial adversity and its consequences are in forming our identities and building our resilience. We also talked about the message we send to others when we solve their problems. The message we send is, "You cannot do this yourself, and you need me." We take away a potential victory and take some of the credit for others doing well. It's much healthier for us to let others own their own struggles, to develop tenacity, and to exercise some self-determination because then they can own their own victories, too, and that's a critical component in building resilience by overcoming adversity.[17] Further, when we take away consequences, people are much more likely to repeat their mistakes.

As parents, it's important to consider this concept when our kids are struggling and we're motivated to "help." I think back to my discussion with Joan, my counselor at AARC, as Sam and Ben neared graduation and my own motives for managing their behaviour. Who are we really helping here? I consider my own trials and what they've taught me about myself. It hasn't been easy but when I've overcome a difficulty, I've felt proud and capable; I've contributed to my sense of self-determination. I'm grateful today for all of the adversity I experienced. It has made me who I am. I'm so grateful I haven't been spared that adversity, that no one stepped in to make my life too smooth. Today, I have the belief that no matter what life throws at me, I'll be okay. The lesson learned is priceless: I've overcome obstacles and come out the other side, stronger and wiser.

A mom who was in treatment at AARC told me she'd do extraordinary things "for" her son. She saw her parenting acrobatics as selfless acts that would benefit her child. I asked her what she was trying to avoid, and she insisted it was "his pain." But I contend that it's really her own pain that she was avoiding. She felt pain seeing him suffer and that's really what all her efforts were about—avoiding her own pain. It hurts to see the people we love struggle or get hurt. This is why we say, "It's hard to love an addict."

Even though we want to save our children from making mistakes, we need to acknowledge that it's those mistakes that can teach them the most valuable lessons about who they are, what they're capable of, and how the world works. This belief was crystalized for me in the summer of 2018.

Sam, Ben, and I planned a road trip to visit my brother and his family in British Columbia. The boys had loved road trips since they were little. It had been a long time since they'd been on a trip like this and a long time since they'd seen their cousins, who were like siblings. As the day to leave came closer, we talked about the details: What time to leave and who would sleep where to minimize delays. (The boys had their own places now, and I lived on my own.) I secretly planned out music and download-ed playlists to my phone. I shopped for the boys' favourite snacks so I could make them snack bags just like they had when they were small.

The day before we were due to leave, I received a call from Ben's girl-friend. She said Ben hadn't come home the night before, which, we all knew, meant he was out using drugs again. I felt my shoulders drop and hung my head as we talked. I paced the front walkway and asked if she was okay, if she needed anything. She was fine, but this meant a change in plans and I appreciated and thanked her for the heads up that Ben had re-lapsed. I hung up and sat down, feeling terribly sad. I said a little prayer to my angels to please keep Ben safe. I reflected on how incredibly powerful addiction was to take over Ben's life only days before an event I knew he was very excited about. It hit me again, that feeling of being robbed of a dream. The excitement we had planning this trip, the visions I had of Ben and Sam opening their snack bags, the music we'd listen to, the laughs we'd have, reminiscent of family road trips we'd taken before. It was all stolen in an instant.

The sun shone brightly that day, and I sat watching happy people walk by my home. I texted Sam to let him know Ben wouldn't be joining us. I also texted Ben to say I loved him. Then with a heavy heart, I began to make the necessary changes to our plans.

As Sam and I drove through the Rocky Mountains the next morning, my thoughts intermittently went to Ben, and I wondered where he was and if he was okay. We drove around treacherous turns in the road which hugged steep cliffs overlooking valleys that seemed to have no bottom. I noted the breathtaking beauty, conscious that one wrong move could send us plummeting to our deaths. Navigating this route safely required me to have my head on straight, focus, and keep my eyes on the horizon. I thought about the pain that Ben would feel as he sobered up and realized he'd missed the trip and the shame he'd feel at having relapsed again. I reflected while I drove that this pattern with Ben had become too familiar, and I knew that when I did hear from him, he'd be sad. He'd apologize, and he'd begin the slow road to recovery through the fog of detox. He'd find his way back to feeling some sense of stability again. Ben and everyone who loved him would end up feeling bruised.

But I realized quite suddenly that even if I could wave my magic wand and take it away, I wouldn't. My temptation to save my kids from pain is more about avoiding my own pain at watching them suffer. I thought back to the times that I'd taught this very concept to parents who were railing against their kids' battles, trying to "fix" things, and the conversations with Joan all those years before. I needed to revisit my attitude and belief about adversity and its capacity to build resilience. I needed to consider again that I demonstrate respect for self-determination through staying out of my kids' business and choosing to look after myself. I needed to let my kids have their struggles.

Today, every now and then, I'm tempted to weigh in on my kids' lives and comment, question, or recommend a direction. It's especially tempting when they present me with a problem or express dissatisfaction with an area of their life. My temptation then is to step right back into trying to take responsibility and direct them. And when I do this, it takes me away from focusing on my own health, of learning to feel what I feel, and take action that's good for me. It's a comfortable place for me, to focus more on others. It saves me from feeling my own discomfort with their struggles.

Having learned repeatedly and to varying degrees that this is damaging to me and the people I love, I've managed to refrain from trying to manage others, for the most part. When I do overstep with uninvited advice, Sam will say something like, "Thanks for trying to arrange my life for me." It's a gentle, lighthearted reminder that I've stepped into his business. I stop and consider what I'm doing and we chuckle a little. And I appreciate it. He reminds me that he's capable of navigating his own life; he doesn't want or need me to step in.

I remind myself that my job is to love my kids, believe in them, and cheer them on. And when I can do this, we are all happier and healthier. Ultimately, stepping in and saving others is a selfish act.

Sam and I had a great time on that trip. And there is freedom in knowing how to find joy with my family, even when another member of our family is struggling.

Reflective Questions:
- When are you tempted to step in and spare your loved one a hardship?
- Are you offering them help because they need it or because you're avoiding the pain of seeing them struggle? Or both?
- Are you taking action they could take for themselves?
- Is your loved one well-resourced if they want help?
- When are you tempted to take on a rescuer role?
- What help are you trying to provide that would be better offered by a qualified professional?

Endnotes

17   https://www.thoughtco.com/self-determination-theory-4628297

https://exploringyourmind.com/resilient-personality-4-defining-features/

CONCLUSION

When I look back at the process of writing this book, I reflect on the discomfort, pain, and embarrassment at admitting some of these truths about myself. At times, I've felt a little whiny and overly dramatic. But mostly, I've felt a deep sense of gratitude for the mental illness and addictions I've experienced within myself and the people I love. They've forced me to change. They broke me and opened me up in ways I would've never experienced had my family and I not travelled this path. I've become a woman with more insight, love, tenderness, and compassion than I would otherwise have had. It's made me less judgmental, more forgiving, and ultimately more spiritual and better connected to myself and others. It has set me on a path to freedom, a path I've been searching for since I was a kid. This has been the gift of my journey with mental health and addictions.

I no longer experience my kids' struggles as a personal trauma. I no longer ride the rollercoaster with them. While they may still experience struggles, I don't experience their pain as my own. I have freedom, joy, and the ability to focus on what's going well. I have a say over my role in my relationships with my kids and that's it. This is not to say that I don't still have to work at staying free. I can easily relapse into codependence and trying to save the day. The difference now is that I am aware of myself slipping into old patterns earlier and know how to get back to myself and live freely again.

I've provided six steps below that you can use on your own journey to freedom. Below each step is my own reflection on those steps and how I think about them today.

1. ***Be sure that you and others have access to professional resources when needed.***
   - I'm confident that my kids are well resourced—they have access to the help that they need and know how to find it. If for any reason I'm unsure of this, or if a new problem arises, I'm ready to offer assistance to help them find the right help. I've learned to shop for help as a "responsible consumer," meaning that I know that not every provider, or every program, is created equal; and I ask questions to help determine what I, or someone I love, needs. I'm not afraid to ask probing questions and take my time. I ensure I'm not making decisions out of fear and frustration but rather that I'm making informed decisions that are intuitively guided. *As tempting as it is, I try* not *to counsel my kids.*
   - Like everyone else, I think I know best how to solve the world's problems, especially my kids'. I'm not short on opinions about what's missing in their lives or what they "need to do" to be happy. My kids know this. And sometimes, they ask for my help. But I work hard to only offer help when asked. I try to be curious, ask more questions, and provide fewer "answers."
   - I check in with myself. If I am struggling, I ask for help. If I need help above and beyond a friendly ear and a reminder to step back from saving my kids, I seek professional help.

2. ***Frequently check in and remind yourself that your loved one has the right to choose their own path through adversity—and get really honest about your motives to "help."***
   - I truly believe that my kids are entitled to their own struggles. And I truly believe (because they've repeatedly demonstrated this) that they're capable of overcoming any hurdle they're ready to work on. I remind them of this with words like, "I know you'll figure this out when you're ready." Before I step in and offer help (making appointments, offering money, driving them somewhere, having them stay with me), I ask myself if I'm willing to be doing this

same thing, or provide this same intervention, forever. If not forever, then how long am I willing to do it? Do they really need this help? Are they capable, and is my temptation to help stemming from my own impatience of discomfort at watching them experience pain? I may ask them what they want for themselves or what they're willing to do to change something if they have a complaint about how their lives are going.

This is helpful for several reasons. It reveals to me whether they're wanting change badly enough to take action or if they're just venting. And it reminds them that they have a choice in how things go. It also helps me to determine their level of commitment to taking action for themselves as opposed to just accepting help from me. One of my boundaries is that I'll only work as hard as someone else when it comes to changing something in their lives. I will not save, rescue, or help someone who isn't willing to do as much or more work for themselves.

3. *Get honest about what's driving your behaviours.*
   - I work on accepting my own fear for my kids, recognizing that it's fear of my own pain and discomfort at witnessing others struggle with addiction and/or relapse. I seek resources to help me accept and process my fears, like professionals or friends. I remind myself that my feelings are normal—they're part of loving other people. I remind myself that no one is "making me feel this way," and in so doing, I remind myself that others are not responsible for changing their behaviours to spare me unpleasant feelings.

4. *Revisit your boundaries each time you feel uneasy and know those boundaries can change.*
   - I consider honestly what's healthy for me, i.e., what's the balance between offering my help and time, and what I need to do for myself to feel joy? Sometimes they're the same thing. There are times when I just really love to offer a helping hand—it brings me joy. But sometimes there's a hidden agenda within me, unspoken conditions I might have around my help and time. Expectations can lead to resentment when not met. If I notice those conditions in play, I dig into them. Do they need to be articulated? Or can I just let them go?

5. *Use validation skills first!*
   - When my kids (or anyone) express to me that they're struggling, I try to make use of validation skills. Preferably, I do this at the beginning of the conversation and then again throughout. I try to relate to the struggle and the feeling they're expressing—fear, sadness, anger, frustration, shame, etc.—and I let them know they're not alone. Only when I think they feel heard do I consider making use of the follow-up questions below.
     - What would you like to see instead?
     - What are you willing to do about that?
     - What help from me would you like? (For me, it's not healthy to put more work into helping my kids than they're willing to put in themselves.)
     - What am I willing to do? This is something I like to discuss with them, offering and then letting go of any expectation (fantasy) about the outcome.
6. *Try to be hard on your opinions and beliefs, and soft on yourself, in the process.*
   - I try to remember that I have opinions and judgments that, over the years, have shifted as I've learned more, had more experiences, and had exposure to things and people that helped open my eyes. I've been wrong so many times. I own my thoughts, opinions, and feelings, and I value a willingness in others to do the same thing. This means, I don't consider my own version of the truth, facts, or reality as objective. I'm open to learning more, to challenging my stories, perspective, and beliefs. In fact, I'm hungry for it. And I'm drawn to others who are the same. I thrive on the connection, understanding, and growth that result.
   - I love all of me. Even the parts of myself that I'm not super proud to admit are there, like the judgemental fearful side. The more I love and accept myself, the more I can love and accept others.

With these points in mind, I've reclaimed my life and my freedom on a very large scale. I've had a ton of support and help in working to change, and I continue to do a lot of work on myself. As I learn more and more about myself—my responses, my reactions, my relationships, and how my past continues to shape my present—I find myself better able to look my problems straight in the eye, with compassion, and then check in with my highest self (often through conversation with good friends). I tell you this because I know without a shadow of a doubt that if you're willing to do the same, there's a true freedom and sense of reclamation available to you too.

Those dashed dreams of 2011 have finally come true. My kids *are* funny, intelligent, and kind people I enjoy spending time with. I hang out with them and laugh; we share the same sense of humour. They're interesting, and I'm so proud to have raised them. I'm thrilled to introduce them to people, and I beam with pride at being their mom. I hold a special place in their hearts and they in mine.

It's 2020 and we are in the mist of the COVID-19 pandemic. As I finish up editing this book, I reflect on my life today. Steve and I are now divorced and I live alone. The kids are all fairly independent, figuring themselves and their lives out, as I expect them to do for the rest of their lives. I have a great relationship with Steve and each of the kids. Spending time with my family is my greatest joy. I live a life of complete freedom and my new normal is working to support other families, hosting a podcast about mental health and resilience called Broken Open, and facilitating leadership development and training. My friends are strong, supportive people, and I have learned to slow down, notice, ask for what I need, take responsibility for caring for myself, and allow others to do the same.

Finally, here's what I know about myself and motherhood today:

I'm a mother who loves spending time with her kids. I love asking questions about what matters to them, what they hope and dream. I enjoy reaffirming my unconditional love and support for them. I'm a mother who loves laughing with her kids. I love when they point out my flaws and tease me about my tendencies. I love watching them laugh together. Time with my kids is my happy place.

I'm a woman who role-models the pursuit of her most authentic and joyful way of living, even if it's against societal norms, traditions, and expectations. I believe that we must ultimately learn to be our most authentic selves in finding joy and meaning in order to be of loving service to each other.

I'm a grandmother and advocate for Athena and any future grandchildren I may have. Further, I'm a strong advocate for all mothers working hard to look after their kids. I love watching mothers and fathers love their kids. These parents have my undying support. I'll stand up for and support parents who are trying—and that includes *you*—always. I'm here to help and support you.

HOPE FOR THE READER
by Sam Towns

I don't remember any traumatic childhood event that so many medical professionals like to use to explain someone's self-destructive behaviour. Today, I chalk my issues up to a low tolerance for emotional distress and discomfort. My drug use and suicide attempts were efforts to escape my feelings of hopelessness, shame, and insecurity.

I used drugs and alcohol from age 14 to 24, and for about half of that time I drank and got high seemingly without consequence. I kept my grades up, was employable, and maintained relationships with family and friends. Using was fun. I had no reason to stop, slow down, or even examine why I was getting blackout drunk or high almost every day.

At age 20, I lost the tight grip I thought I had over every aspect of my life. I attempted suicide when I was drunk in the summer after my second year of university. Days later, I had a psychotic break and landed myself in the hospital for three weeks. My thinking was delusional and paranoid. It didn't return to normal for over a year. I couldn't keep a part-time job. I couldn't pass all my courses when I decided to return to school for a semester. My relationships with family and friends were crumbling. And I had a few more suicide attempts.

I believed my own brain chemistry had suddenly betrayed me. I thought there was nothing I could do; I was the victim of circumstances beyond my control. It wasn't until I was 21, a year and a half after my first suicide attempt, that I fully accepted that my chronic alcohol and drug use were primarily to blame for what I was experiencing.

Even then, with full knowledge and awareness of what I was doing, I'd make the choice to use after a period of sobriety. The need to escape my own thoughts and feelings was so strong, it overpowered my rational thoughts of self-preservation. I used drugs and attempted suicide even after I'd experienced freedom from my addiction and knew there was hope.

Today, I've been free of the most obvious self-destructive behaviours, like drug use and suicide attempts, for over two years. This isn't the result of one event or treatment model. My cumulative knowledge, experience, and personal circumstances are the reasons for my success in consistently choosing not to run from my uncomfortable emotions and instead face them head-on. I have a supportive family, knowledge of resources in my community, and a willingness to grow and seek personal freedom.

I know that I'll never be completely out of the woods. For all I know, by the time you're reading this, I'll have relapsed into my old pattern of behaviour. But today, as I write this, I have the freedom to choose to be present and live a full life. I have hope to share with the reader.

FLOODS OF DOPAMINE
by Ben Towns

It only took me about eight years to finally admit I had a drug problem. From ages 12 to 20, I thought that life was a party and that the party must be had. It wasn't until I was smoking meth on the streets of downtown Calgary that I admitted to myself I was addicted.

When I was 18 and living in my van, I felt free. No more nagging parents, just some drugs and some friends. I thought, hey, time for a November campout!

I've always loved my parents, and I never wanted to disappoint them, but I had to feel what I was missing, the flood of dopamine in my brain. Nothing was going to take me away from what I loved at the time.

Today, I'm almost nine months sober.

If you asked why or how, I'd say that there are countless reasons, influences, and experiences that helped me along the way.

I don't want to die young. I want my daughter to grow up with a father. I still want to achieve my life goals and do amazing things. Just for today, that's my plan.

MISERY IN SOLITUDE
by Sydney Towns

To be perfectly honest, my memories of those years of family chaos and recovery are a blur. For the most part, I was sad and lonely and angry. I felt bitterness towards my siblings for disrupting the family dynamic that we'd established in our childhoods. I felt naïve when memories with my brothers gradually got tainted by the realization that they weren't as happy and substance-free as I thought. And I felt like I'd lost all the people I'd grown closest to.

Most of my time was spent dealing with the internal battle of wanting to be noticed by my parents but not wanting to feel like another burden. It was confusing because it seemed that the more "trouble" my siblings caused, the more love and resources they got and the less there was for me. I ended up fantasizing about getting in an accident or being the target of a violent attack so I could be the centre of attention. My own mental health became an issue, and I suffered from nearly debilitating social anxiety and depression, but I told myself my problems were never bad enough. I wanted to be alone all the time, in my room or driving around in my car, both activities that alienated me from everyone even more—both of which only made me feel worse.

I childishly let myself wallow in self-pity, but at the time I thought isolation was my version of self-care; in reality, it was just another way of staying under the radar and resisting help. Having to do even the smallest things outside of my tiny comfort zone would bring me to tears. I wasn't blameless when it came to any of my problems, but I let myself feel like a victim of my family and my mental illness.

When I look back, I feel gratitude. I credit those years for maturing me emotionally and bringing me out of my shell. I have so much love for all of my family and boundless respect for each of their journeys.

FICKLE AND FRONTING
by Ally Towns

When I was young, I liked the feeling of collecting things. I didn't always like the things that I collected, but I liked to pick up rocks, coins, shells, and leaves, and I'd put them on my dresser, tape them to pages of a journal, or put them in Tupperware containers in my closet. I'd have my friends over and show them my collections of boring things in the hopes they'd see a personality trait in me I didn't fully believe I had. Yes, I see beauty in mundane things! I wasn't putting rocks or leaves on display; I was putting an idea of who I wanted to be on display. I was a person that collected things.

Later, I watched all of my peers go through confirmation, a commitment to the Catholic faith I didn't fully understand. I went to confirmation, then fully engulfed myself in the faith. I created a prayer corner in my room, prayed every night, and read a children's Bible front to back several times. In an effort to become "holier," I even *drank* from a small bottle of holy water that was gifted to me upon my confirmation. I was a person who had (maybe too much) faith.

Fast forward to the age of 13, and I wanted everything to be pink. Pink stuffed animals, pink walls, pink blankets, pink clothes. I was a person who loved pink!

This went on and on and on. I didn't believe in all of it. I knew I was lying to myself. The reality of it is this: I felt hollow. I was devoid of personality, but I saw people who had personality and I wanted to own myself like they did. I didn't start thinking my "personality fashion shows" were strange until grade nine. My fellow students were growing into themselves. They became more confrontational, expressed their interests, and called things like they were. I became a person who felt deeply sad but this time I was not trying it on for size. It was true.

My self-harming was difficult to explain to my parents and, strangely, even more difficult to explain to my friends. I was very outgoing with them but I wore my pain under my sleeves. I didn't have the words to tell my friends what I was feeling, but I did have the words to tell them what was going on at home with my brothers. They understandably distanced themselves, as did my boyfriend at the time, despite any manipulation I threw their way.

As for my mom and dad, I saw how much I scared them and their frustration with me was apparent. I recognized that they often saw me as a roadblock in their journey to saving Sam and Ben. My self-harm wasn't nearly as serious as their addictions, their rehab, or their suicidal behaviour. On the days I didn't feel like a roadblock, I felt like a juggled ball.

I didn't need rehab. I didn't need to leave the house. I didn't need the psych ward. I needed cognitive behavioural therapy. I needed to see my school counsellor. I needed dialectical behaviour therapy (DBT). I needed medication, but more importantly, I needed my mom and dad on my side. I so badly wanted to be heard, to be acknowledged.

When I was in high school, I finally found a therapist I connected with. She's a psychologist who specialises in DBT, and for the first time in years I felt completely understood by someone. She knew everything about me—the good *and* the bad—and still treated me like a friend. Sitting across from her, under a blanket, clasping a hot chocolate, I would tell her the ugliest things about myself. The sessions were all about me, how I was doing, crazy high school drama, drama at home. I was mindful that she was being paid handsomely to listen to me and offer validation and "homework," but it meant the world to be heard out by an adult.

One day, later in my high school years, my mom saw some fresh cuts on my arm. I've always felt like that's a mom thing: Doing a full subconscious scan of their kids every time they see them. My daily mom-scan showed a sign of distress and she asked me about it. I gave her the rundown, "I cut last night; I was feeling sad." To my surprise, there was no "What did you use," "Why weren't you sleeping," or "It's disturbing to look at." She simply said, "Is there anything I can do to help you?" In my shock, I told her that I was fine—it was just a blip.

Whenever I think about the moment that my mom let go of her anger and replaced it with support, I remember a day in grade four. My friends had ditched me. I came home after school and explained what happened to my mom through pouring tears. She sat on the couch and cradled me on her lap. I was curled up in her arms, crying all over her sweater and feeling the gentle rocking motion she made as she whispered validation to me, "Grade four is hard. Your brothers and sister struggled through grade four too."

It was the validation, the acknowledgement. She was powerless over my friends ditching me or what happened the next day at school but the validation that it was *hard for me* meant everything. Grade four is *hard.* Mental illness is *hard.* Using the proper coping mechanisms is *hard.* I think that my mom, if she'd been my age and in my position, would've told those girls off. But years and years and years later, she held her teary eyed, eight-year-old girl and told her that she saw real pain in the struggle of being a kid. I felt like the strongest kid in the world after that and it wasn't the holy water I drank.

When I think back, I remember plenty of doctors' visits, psychiatric visits, psychologist visits, and lots of therapy. To the majority of adults in my life, I was seen as a patient. Much of the time we all focused on my mental illness. As a result, when I finally received a diagnosis, it became the biggest identifier for who I was and how I saw myself. Later, when my parents said things like, "You are insightful," "You are wise," "You are unique," "You're such a good girl," I began to feel human again; I began to see myself as more than just a patient with an illness. My idea of who I was, was finally coming together.

Today, I know that I want to help others who struggle. I want to help them to see themselves as humans who are more than their illnesses. I am excited to be attending university to pursue a career in Child and Youth Care Counselling.

I'm a person who doesn't self-harm. I'm a person who loves music. I'm a person who has a job. I'm a person with loving, healthy friends. I'm a person with a smart boyfriend. I'm a person with a drive to succeed. I'm a person who loves her family and loves to spend time with them.

I'm a happy person with a thirst for life.

ACKNOWLEDGEMENTS

I have so many people to thank. Countless people have contributed to this book, both directly and indirectly. I'll start with my family. Thank you, Steve, Sam, Ben, Sydney, and Ally, for sharing the journey and giving me permission to use your experiences to provide context in telling my story. You've been so generous in allowing me to recount our struggles in an effort to help other people. You've seen me at my best and worst as a mom and a wife and you've help to shape me into a better person. I love you and admire each of you in a very special way.

Thanks, too, to my siblings, who've given me permission to disclose how our family of origin affected me. Thank you to my book coaches, Les Kletke and Tammy Plunkett. Les, you were the first to read my very, very raw account of my childhood in my first drafts and you handled it beautifully. I'll always be grateful. And your encouragement and faith stuck with me until I could write a book that I actually want to publish—this one! Tammy, you helped me shape this book—finally. It's been in me and had several iterations over the years. You took my call, made time, sat down with me, and helped me organize my thoughts. You got what I was trying to do! Thank you for your help and your words of encouragement. Telling me that this book is needed and that it will help others, kept me going when I felt overwhelmed. Amanda Myrfield, thanks for your infinite patience. You've been waiting for me to finish this for years! You stuck with me and facilitated the editorial process. Thank you for your help in getting this book ready for the world and for getting it out there.

Huge thanks to Paul Carlucci, my editor. At times, you seemed to understand better than I did what I was trying to say. Thank you for "getting it" and for being so darned quick, so encouraging, and so effective at communicating! You're amazing at what you do! Thank you to the group at Book Launchers for helping me in the final stages of making my book sellable.

I thought often, while writing, of a quote by Isaac Newton in which he said, "I stand on the shoulders of giants." I consider that whenever I think of anything I know and anything I've learned. I give credit and thanks to those who came before me and those who were willing to prop me up, give me hope, teach me, support me, encourage me, and walk with me through my life. To that end, thank you to Dr. Dean Vause, the creator and executive director of AARC, the program that launched our family into recovery. Special thanks to the other mothers and professionals I met at AARC, especially Joan, Natalie, Brenda, and Jackie. You're incredible women, and you've all had a profound impact on my life.

Thank you to the staff at my favourite Starbucks in Bridgeland, who kept me caffeinated and entertained while I wrote!

And finally, thank you to my clients, in both nursing and consulting. You've let me into your lives and allowed me to witness your most private struggles. It's been my privilege. You've taught me valuable lessons, and I'm honoured to have walked with you for a brief time.

CPSIA information can be obtained
at www.ICGtesting.com
Printed in the USA
LVHW050551060121
675802LV00022B/593

9 780994 856692